Adventures in Living Consciously

Deborah Alyne Christy

Adventures in Living Consciously

How I learned to live in the present with purpose and self-awareness while navigating life's mine fields.

Deborah Alyne Christy

A Bountiful Life Coaching
Coeur d'Alene, Idaho

Acknowledgements

"We can't become what we need to be by remaining what we are." Oprah Winfrey

There are so many who have guided me along my way, but in particular I would like to thank:

Steve Greene and Theodora Sallee for their long-standing and unending friendship, guidance, and love.

My mom, dad, and brothers who have always loved me unconditionally.

My cousin, Karen Orchard for her love and friendship.

My best friend and soul sister, Darlene Brueggeman.

Donald Barker for his guidance and friendship.

Jackie and Dieter Gedeik for their guidance and assistance.

Landmark Education.

Zoetha Amritam and her teachings.

Table of Contents

One of them tempts us—ah! what a dream, to live in that!—the other stifles us at the first breath." Colette

"The will is never free—it is always attached to an object, a purpose. It is simply the engine in the car—it can't steer." Joyce Cary

"If you have abandoned one faith, do not abandon all faith. There is always an alternative to the faith we lose. Or is it the same faith under another mask?" Graham Greene

"He who knows others is clever; He who knows himself has discernment." Lao-Tzu

"When you have to make a choice and don't make it, that in itself is a choice." William James

"Half the work that is done in this world is to make things appear what they are not." Elias Root Beadle

"The purpose of life is to live it, to taste
    experience to the utmost, to reach out
    eagerly and without fear for newer and
    richer experience." Eleanor Roosevelt

Chapter 1

"The truth is out there." The X-Files

People are gathering on a grassy knoll overlooking Lake Coeur d'Alene as dawn explodes in brilliant hues of red and orange against a deep indigo sky. Even though it is very early, there is a sizeable group of people gathering for this unusual meeting.

Early morning still has a chill to it, even though it's August and the height of summer. There is a feeling of restless anticipation as we find a place to sit and wait for the arrival of Johanna. Everyone is preparing their spot with blankets, towels, or beach chairs.

I sit on my towel and lightly run my hand over the dewy grass and gaze to the east as the sun majestically rises above the mountains. I think back to the day I heard about Johanna and marvel at being at the right place at the right time. It all started with a heated conversation I overheard.

I was on the beach at Hayden Lake when a man and woman in their late twenties rode up on their bikes. I was sitting on the shore looking out at the lake and they stopped off to my right. They leaned their bikes against a maple tree, put their helmets on their handlebars, and walked toward the water. They were talking quietly. I turned my face up to the sun and enjoyed its warmth. After about 10 minutes, the couple started to argue as they were walking back to their bikes.

The man was fair skinned with freckles and strawberry blonde hair. The woman was pretty, with jet-black hair and tanned skin.

"How can you be so gullible?" The man was saying. "There is no such thing as a messiah or master or whatever you want to call it... especially not a woman!"

The woman's face reddened as she fought off her rage. "Oh great — not only is there no such person, but even if there could be, she definitely couldn't be a woman. I thought I knew you. I thought we were friends. But how can we be when I am so obviously beneath you?"

I glanced over as the man's face twisted in anger. "I never said that! You're putting words in my mouth! How can I talk to you when you act so self-righteous?"

The man stopped and sighed as the woman looked at him with her mouth open. She didn't say a word. She looked totally dumbfounded and very hurt.

"If you want me to go, Jeannie, I will. I can

meet you at Lake City Park in the morning."

"Don't do me any favors, Roy. I don't need to be patronized." With that, the woman grabbed her bike, slammed on her helmet and stormed off. Once she was off the grass she mounted her bike and raced away with the man trailing after her, calling her name.

"A messiah?" I thought to myself. "This I've got to see."

➡

A sudden rush of whispers brings me back to the present as a woman in a plain, white, calf-length dress approaches the top of the knoll. Her long blonde hair radiates the colors of the sunrise.

There is an immediate silence as the woman walks around the group and smiles at every person one by one. When her eyes look into mine, I get butterflies in my stomach and I feel that I'm in the presence of a very special person. It's as though a soft glowing light shines within her. Her face is pretty and gentle, yet plain all at the same time. Her complexion is light and she has several rows of freckles across her nose. Her deep blue eyes take me aback.

Suddenly, I feel light and peaceful. A feeling I can only describe as 'a sense of belonging' that

I have experienced only a few times in my life. It's as though I have been filled with intense love. I return her smile and wonder if this is the person the woman in the park was speaking about.

The woman moves to the front of the group. We are spread out all around the knoll. Her voice is gentle and loving. "My name is Johanna. I suggest you move into a semicircle over here," she says as she points to the area directly in front of her.

With a flurry of whispers and movements we are soon in a semicircle and Johanna sits in front of us. I notice the woman from the park yesterday is here without her friend.

"Welcome. I am so pleased to be here with you. I know that each of you has come for a particular reason… even if you aren't aware of it. Most of you are here because of a nagging feeling — an intuition that there is more to your life than your day-to-day activities. Am I correct?"

Most of us nod, a few shrug, and others just stare at her. I can sense feelings of embarrassment, uneasiness, and even anger in this group of about twenty men and women.

"Well," Johanna continues, "**I** say you are all here for the **same** reason. You might be here to be healed of a physical ailment. You might be here to get rid of an emotional trauma or to learn how to be abundant. Maybe you're here out of curiosity or because you want to prove that I'm a phony. However, make no mistake—you are all here for one reason. Each of you wants to know the truth.

"I don't mean Jan's truth or John's truth or the church's truth or your doctor's truth. I don't mean your husband's or your wife's truth. There is no 'your truth' or 'my truth.' There is only one truth. It's the truth that sleeps beneath all your questions and troubles. The one that can set every person free and it's yours for the taking.

"There *is* a catch, however. Truth can't be given to you or forced on you. You must be willing to see and accept it. I can't do it for you. You have to want this with every fiber of your being. Truth requires that you take responsibility for the issues in your life and stop blaming other people or situations. You will need to recognize all of the ways you create your present existence.

"You see, I can help you overcome a gripping disease or an intense psychological trauma. However, you won't be able to stay healthy unless you are willing to do two things: look for truth in every area of your life, and face your deepest fears. This may sound easy, but keep in mind that fear is what caused your distress, or dis-ease, to begin with.

"Fear can twist your body or your mind in a devastating way. Few people realize that fear is the foundation of their problems. They go from doctor to doctor and can't understand why they don't stay healthy. Remember this: pills can only treat your symptoms; they do not have the power to heal your emotional traumas. It takes courage and dedication to truth to overcome and truly heal.

"I am devoted to truth. I am here to help anyone who truly desires to be free. 'Free of what?' you may ask. Free of emotional or physical pain. Free of fear. Once you are free of fear, you are then free to live a life of health, peace, and joy. Free to live in the highest spiritual truth possible. Free to be.

"But, I must warn you — in order to live without fear you must be willing to slay your dragons every day. There will always be something in your life that tugs at you and threatens your ability to be present. It could be an argument with a loved one, losing your job, injuries to your body, the loss of someone dear to you, and so on. You will need to face each trauma and learn not to be destroyed by them; and that can be very challenging, indeed. I am willing to share ways of overcoming these issues for anyone who is interested.

Johanna stops and smiles at the group. "If what I have said bothers any of you, then this would be a good time for you to leave."

As Johanna pauses to give people the

opportunity to leave, we all look around to one another, but no one leaves. Our attention turns back to Johanna who is still smiling, and as the sun continues to ascend behind her, the light radiates around her and she looks like she is glowing. It is so intense that my eyes begin to water and I have to look away. Johanna stands and walks around us. She stops right in front of me, lowers herself to one knee, and touches my chin. She looks in my eyes and her hand is warm — really warm. I feel tense, excited, and a little afraid. I can feel her looking deep within me.

"What is your name?"

"Deborah," I say, quivering for no apparent reason.

"Welcome, beloved Deborah. I can see you have worked long and hard at seeking the truth and vanquishing your fears."

"How can you know that?" I am stunned by her accuracy. I have been on a path of self-discovery for years.

"I can see it. But know this: your work is not yet finished. There will be a time of great strife and you will be taken to the limits of your fear and pain. Remember who you are and you will do fine." That's all she says. Then she stands and walks up to a woman who has her head bent. Johanna kneels in front of her and touches her chin in the same way. The woman looks at her with tears in her eyes. It's the woman I saw arguing in town yesterday.

"I know of your pain," Johanna starts. "I know your father has hurt you deeply."

The woman jumps and her eyes become wide with fear and amazement. She stammers her reply. "H-how can you possibly know that?"

Johanna's gentle smile is filled with compassion. "Do you wish to be free of this pain?"

"Y-yes. Yes, of course, but it's impossible. I have tried for years. I've seen doctors and counselors, but nothing helps." The woman wipes her eyes with the back of her hands.

"Then come and sit with me. We will walk through your pain together." Johanna and the woman walk hand in hand to the front of the group and sit down.

"What is your name?"

"Jeannie. Jeannie Carr."

"Well, Jeannie, let me explain something to you. I can't 'fix' you. If you truly want to be free of the pain you have been carrying around since you were a child, then you must be willing to face your fear. This means that before I can help you release your pain you will have to relive it again. The difference is that you will not run from it this time. This type of courage and honesty reveals the true nature of the experience to you. Are you willing to go on?"

"I-I think so." Jeannie is biting her lip, searching within for what she wants to do. "Yes," she says, finally, "yes I will do whatever it takes to stop feeling like this."

"Good. Close your eyes and take a deep breath. Let it out slowly and feel yourself relax. Good. Now continue to take deep, slow breaths. With each breath you feel yourself relax more and more. Every breath releases tension in your muscles."

Jeannie takes several deep breaths but is obviously not relaxing. Johanna places her hand on Jeannie's shoulder and talks gently to her. I can't hear what she is saying, but as she talks, Jeannie begins to relax. Johanna helps her lie down on the grass. She tells Jeannie to open her throat and breathe directly into her chest. Her breath sounds rough. Her body is twitching slightly and she is grimacing, as though she is very uncomfortable.

Is she remembering something unpleasant or is she merely trying to get comfortable?

Johanna places her left hand a few inches above Jeannie's body at her navel and the other just above the top of her head. Jeannie starts to groan and her movements are increasing.

Johanna speaks softly. "That's right. Allow yourself to remember. Allow yourself to see. Look into the eyes of your father and feel the terror." Johanna's left hand moves up Jeannie's body and stops just above her heart.

Jeannie's body jerks and her head is rolling from side to side. I scream in my mind, '*She doesn't want to remember*.' She doesn't want to look at her father. Suddenly, she stops moving entirely and her body relaxes so much that I wonder if she has passed out. My concern for this stranger is overwhelming and I don't know why.

"You have played out your entire childhood drama," Johanna softly states. "Now you can make the conscious choice to forgive all of the players, including yourself. Can you forgive your father, Jeannie? Can you truly forgive him for all he has done to you?"

"I… I don't know. I feel so angry."

"What is the source of your anger?"

"What do you mean?"

"What feelings do you associate with your father's treatment of you as a child?"

"I was constantly afraid of him."

"Close your eyes again. I want you to view your childhood as though you are viewing snapshots. Start with your earliest memory of your father and freeze the picture. How old are you and what is the feeling?"

"I am about two or three and I feel love, happiness, and admiration."

"Next snapshot?"

"I am around seven and I feel scared. I don't want to make dad angry, because he spanks hard."

"Next?"

"I'm thirteen. I avoid dad whenever I can. I try very hard never to be left alone with him. When I am alone with him I feel terrified that I might do something to make him mad.

"One night when I was 15, mom was sick and I was trying to make dinner. I spilled the milk and dad flew into a rage, throwing his beer across the kitchen. He slapped me and then made me clean up the milk *and* his beer while he drank a new one in the living room. I was so scared and confused… I didn't know what I did that was so terrible. All I was trying to do was to help out while mom was sick. I… I remember that when I stopped crying I was sure I could hear mom crying in the bedroom."

"And the next?"

"I'm seventeen and I like a boy in my class. Dad doesn't like him and he forbade me to see him. I saw him anyway and dad found out. He screamed at me and grounded me for two months. I was nearly 18 and very angry, so I started to argue with him. He raised his fist to slug me for talking back and mom jumped to my defense. She's never stepped in before, and I could see she was scared, but she did it anyway.

She did it for me.

He started to beat her and throw her around like a rag doll. He was beating her up so badly that I ran out and called the police from the neighbor's house."

Jeannie's hands are fists. Her eyes are scrunched closed and there are tears slipping down the side of her face as she lies on the grass and tells her awful story.

"What happened next, Jeannie?" Johanna asks quietly.

"The police arrested dad and the ambulance was called to take mom to the hospital. She nearly died and she was still too scared to stand up to him and press charges. This kind of stuff went on for years and she just took it. Just before they released her from the hospital she finally pressed charges and dad finally got what he deserved—he went to prison. Mom divorced him and we moved away.

The anger is creeping back into Jeannie's voice, "Because of him, we moved far away from my friends, my home town, and my boyfriend."

Johanna begins to speak slowly to Jeannie, but she is clearly addressing all of us. "Behind every feeling of anger is another emotion. Once you can understand the nature of your anger you can learn to let go of your past. Jeannie, you said you are angry with your father. Why are you angry?"

"Because he hit me!"

"What were you feeling when you thought he would hit you?"

"I was afraid."

"Yes! Anger is caused by fear. Think about it." Johanna looks around at the group. "Look behind the anger you feel and you will find fear. You are angry with your child because she came home late translates into—you are afraid something has happened to her. You are angry with your mate because he forgets your anniversary translates into—you are afraid he doesn't love you.

"But know this: all fear comes from one place within you. It is the fear of death. You become angry because you fear the death of yourself or of someone or something you love. Jeannie, what would it take for you to forgive your father?"

Jeannie sits up and yells right in Johanna's face, **"How can I ever forgive him? He was a monster to us!"**

She dramatically fights off her tears by gulping huge breaths of air. Johanna places her palm over Jeannie's heart.

"How does your anger serve you?"

Jeannie breaks down in heavy sobs, hiding her face in her hands. Johanna asks the question again.

"How does your anger serve you? What benefits do you derive from it?"

As Jeannie fights for breath, she whispers hoarsely, "None." She stops crying by taking huge gulps of air again, trying to calm herself.

"That's right. There are no benefits from anger or fear. You may feel a sense of satisfaction at hating someone or getting back in anger, but the only one you hurt is yourself."

Johanna scans the crowd. "Is Jeannie's father sitting here crying? Is *he* suffering from the anger and fear? No! Jeannie is here. She is the one who is suffering. Do you see? The ones that hurt you are not the ones who suffer. You suffer every time you relive the past or create a set of behaviors based on past experiences. The past is the past, but you carry it around, dragging it behind you. Then as you gain new experiences, you take the ones that hurt you and add them to all that baggage you are dragging behind you. The past grows bigger and bigger and becomes so big that it spills over into your present experiences, and invisibly colors your life.

"Jeannie, tell me about your father's childhood. What was it like for him as a boy?"

Jeannie is calmer now, slowing her breathing, and wiping her eyes with her hands. "I really don't know that much about it. Dad said that his father was really strict. I remember that grandma never spoke when grandpa was talking, and that she was a sweet and loving lady. The biggest thing I remember about grandma, other than her great cooking, was that she was really clumsy. She always had bruises or bandages. She said it was because she got dizzy and fell down a lot. I always thought that she had some terrible disease and didn't want me to know.

"I never saw grandpa drink, but I remember hearing rumors that he had a still hidden in the woods somewhere. I never spent much time at grandma and grandpa's since they lived so far away. We only visited them three or four times the whole time I was growing up."

Johanna nods and then says, "Do *you* think your grandma was clumsy?"

"Well, I never saw her get dizzy or bump into things, but she always said…." Jeannie's face drained of color and she looked at Johanna with shock and pain. "Oh no! Not grandpa, too! Are you saying that he beat grandma?"

"Where do you think your father got his temper? When did it begin? What do you think caused him to be *so* afraid that he was angry so much of his life?"

"I always thought he was just mean. But I remember pictures of mom and dad when they were young and they always looked so happy together. Then I figured dad was always mad because of me." Jeannie gazes off, lost in thought.

No one says a word the whole time she is thinking. It's almost as if we are all collectively holding our breath, hoping she will see the connection. Why is it always easier to see someone else's answers to life's difficulties than our own?

Johanna speaks so softly, that I have to strain to hear her say, "Do you think your grandfather abused your dad and his mother?"

Jeannie looks up, astounded at the discovery. "Yes! I think he *did*!"

"Do you know that almost all abusive behavior is learned within the family unit? Every child is the product of their environment; their parents' beliefs and actions mold them in invisible, permanent ways. Only when people understand this and face the programming they received in their youth can they learn to change those aspects that do not serve them.

"You have lived in an abusive home, just as your father did. You have the same history. You have the capacity to repeat the abusive behavior to your children. Or you might marry a man like your father, which is very common."

Jeannie is shaking her head and raising her voice at Johanna's words. "No... NO... **NO**... **NO! I won't allow it! Not again.**" Her voice steadies as she continues. "I already brought a man into my life that was abusive and I finally got away from him after a two-year relationship."

"How can you stop it?"

"I don't know, but I will. I will do whatever it takes to break that pattern of abuse I've lived with all my life. Johanna, please tell me what I need to do. How do I survive my father's influence so I don't continue to create violence in my life?"

"I already have."

"You have? Tell me again, Johanna, please tell me again,"

"You need to start by forgiving your father." As she makes the statement, Jeannie looks down.

Johanna continues: "It's easier to forgive him than you might think. First, think about him as a boy. He was an innocent child, looking to his parents for guidance. What he learns from his father is that if he is in control, he won't have to feel fear. His father's behavior teaches him that drinking and beating the family is manly. He is taught, through experience, that he must be the head of the family unit by keeping everyone in line. He must mete out punishment as his father did, and *his* father before him.

"Jeannie, your father did the best he could with the tools he had. It wasn't entirely his fault. He knew it wasn't right, but he couldn't stop his rage — he didn't know how. Part of his behavior was retaliation. He was enraged with his father, his childhood, and his life. He spent most of his childhood in fear of his father."

"I can see that, but I don't see why he had to take it out on us." Jeannie sighs. "I don't know how to let go of this pain."

"Are you ready to be free of the pain?"

"Yes, of course! Is it really possible?"

"Yes."

"But I always thought it took years of anger and grief work before anyone can release traumatic events. That's why I haven't faced it before now."

"It does not need to take years. You can achieve peace in minutes, not years."

"But how, Johanna?"

"Follow my guidance and I will show you. Lie back down and close your eyes. Breathe fully from your diaphragm and not from your chest. Good. Feel yourself relaxing with each breath. Go to your special place… the one that lets you feel safe. You used to go there as a young girl. Feel the woods around you. Smell the moss and dampness. See the birds and animals as you watch silently from the limb of the great pine tree you loved so much."

Jeannie's breathing slows and her body relaxes. There's a smile on her face as she visits her special place. I find myself wondering how

Johanna knows of Jeannie's special place.

"Good, now imagine the scene that I describe to you. See yourself as the ten-year-old girl you were, escaping your pain and confusion by visiting those woods.

A boy enters the woods in front of you. He doesn't see you. He picks up a dead branch and walks with it. Suddenly, he stops in front of a tree, and with deep, painful screams he begins to beat the tree with the branch. The branch breaks and he stops. With sagging shoulders, he plops down beneath the tree and begins to cry softly. He has a bloody nose and his shirt is torn. You realize the blood and torn shirt aren't from beating the tree. You feel so sorry for him that you want to go and comfort him. You know he would probably be embarrassed, so you gather all of the love and peace you receive from these woods, and you send it to him like a wave of light.

"As you send love to the boy, you notice he has stopped crying. He starts to look around at the woods and wildlife, and you can tell he feels better. He looks surprised when he sees you in the tree. Say hello and smile at him. Hear him say hello back. He gets up and walks over to you. Jump down from the tree and sit beneath it. As he sits down, you ask him if he got into a fight. He looks down at the ground and shakes his head…"

"So what happened to you? Did you fall?"

"Nah, I'm too good of a hiker for that," he says, fidgeting with the twigs and leaves on the ground.

"If you don't want to talk about it, I understand."

"It…it's my old man. He knocks me around when I do something bad."

"Your dad did that to you? That's not right. He shouldn't hurt you like that."

"Aww, it's nothin'. I barely feel it," he brags, puffing out his chest.

"Yeah, right. I sure would feel it. What'd you do that made him so mad?"

"I dunno. I came home from school an' he said I didn't do my chores right last night. He's been awfully mad lately. I hear him tell mom that the money from the crops won't be good enough to pay all our bills again this year. He goes for these long walks in the woods durin' the day an' when he comes home he ain't walkin' right."

"That's terrible. What's wrong with him? Is he sick?"

"I dunno," he shrugs, "but it seems like he comes home even madder."

"Oh. My name is Jeannie, what's yours?"

"Ernie."

Jeannie's eyes snap open and she looks at Johanna. "That's my dad's name!"

"I know. You have just met your father as a boy. Do you hate that boy?"

"Of course not."

"Do you feel anger toward that boy in the woods?"

"No. I felt sorry for him."

Johanna sighs softly and nods. "That is the beginning of forgiveness. Keep working with that boy when you have a quiet moment or when your feelings of anger toward your father surface. Walk through your feelings, one by one. When you reach a place where you can truly forgive your father, then I want you to begin the work of forgiving your mother."

"My *mother*? I don't understand."

"Yes. Didn't you used to feel angry with your mother for not sticking up for you when you were younger? And as you grew, weren't you angry with her for not leaving your father and taking you away from him?"

Jeannie nods silently as Johanna asks each question.

"And the night she was beaten in front of you, weren't you angry with **yourself** for blaming your mom?"

Jeannie nods again as she grabs her stomach with one hand and covers her mouth with the other. Tears start rolling down her cheeks at the picture of her dad beating her mom.

"You can forgive your mother by talking to her and asking her all of the questions you have stuffed deep inside of you. Ask her about *her* childhood. Get to know your mother and the things that make her the person she is.

"Then, finally, you must forgive yourself."

"Myself? For what?"

"You must forgive yourself for your anger toward your mother that later turned into guilt when she nearly died saving you from your father. Forgive yourself for being in that situation and being helpless.

"You have chosen at every twist and turn of your life what experiences you will have. Even the act of not making a decision is a choice. Every person in your life has crossed your path for a reason. There are no accidents. Now it's time you forgive yourself for creating the person you are now from your severe life experiences. You can forgive yourself for not knowing how to be what your father wanted you to be. You can forgive yourself for drawing a mirror image of your father into your first long-term relationship. You can forgive yourself for being afraid.

"Forgiveness does not have to take a lifetime. Healing does not need to take years. You can choose to forgive and heal right now and never have to feel the agony again. The requirements for this kind of healing are the conscious desire to be free and the ability to understand the lesson behind the experience. We all come into this world with an understanding of the things we will experience. In essence, you chose your experiences. You all choose moment by moment how your world will unfold. And then, you choose to chain those experiences to you and drag them through your life. To truly heal, you must first accept responsibility for everything you are and have been creating."

Jeannie closes her eyes slowly and tries to grasp everything Johanna has told her. Before she can respond, a man in the audience yells, "So, are you saying that **she** created her father's abuse-- that it was **her** fault that he was violent?"

I recognize the man as he stands up from the very back of the group. It's Roy, the one who was arguing with Jeannie yesterday.

Johanna answers his anger with patience. "There is no fault or blame. No right or wrong. Every human being is born innocent and carefree. As we create and live our life experiences, we begin collecting baggage. We wrap this baggage around our hearts and minds so tightly that we end up cutting off love and coloring our future with the past.

"You have steeped yourselves in the illusion that everything happens randomly and you have no control over the outcome." Johanna turns back to Jeannie, who is looking both terrified and furious at Roy's outburst. "Jeannie, close your eyes again and take a deep breath. Focus on your past. Can you give me one example of how you created your life based on your past?"

After about two minutes, Jeannie opens her eyes and sits up. "Are you saying that I *chose* my last boyfriend so I could continue to live in a violent home?"

"Perhaps," Johanna nods.

"Why would anyone…why would I choose that?"

"Humans tend to create futures based on their pasts. Even if the past is terrible, they will recreate it over and over again. This occurs partly because it is familiar, partly because it is safer than the unknown, and partly because they feel it is all they deserve. But once the truth is known, you can finally realize that who you are today is the result of what you have thought about yourself and what you think about life."

"If I understand you, Johanna, then you're saying that I'm not my past?"

"Yes, but there is more. The underlying factor is that most of you have forgotten who you are. You have become separated from the truth. You spend so much time in your past and so much energy trying to live into your future, that you are not creating NOW. Your past creates your beliefs, your future creates your fears, and there in no present. You are not... being... present.

"And you have forgotten that you are all connected to one another and to all living things. You affect each other and don't even notice. You scare each other and think it's normal. You live in darkness and think it is light. Think of life like this: each life form is a thread that when woven together make up a beautiful tapestry and the name of that tapestry is Love. If you remove threads from a tapestry, does it maintain its fluidity and beauty?" She scans the group and answers her own question. "No. Removing threads causes the tapestry to look uneven...not whole.

⬅

My mind starts moving back in time and I am remembering my own childhood. I remember how difficult things were for me and how I never felt as though I belonged. I could never grasp what that meant, but I took it as meaning I wasn't supposed to be alive and I acted on that belief several times.

When I was five years old we lived in Los Angeles. My parents were having problems and my dad left us for several months. I was devastated and believed that it was somehow my fault. Mom had to go to work after he left and I was left in day care all morning and with one of my brothers the rest of the afternoon.

When my mom got home at night, she was exhausted and I was starved for her attention. I felt abandoned and alone. One day, I lay down on the sidewalk and closed my eyes to see if anyone would notice me. When a car slowed and the female passenger rolled down her window and asked, "Are you all right?" I jumped up and ran away. I was so shocked that I was actually noticed.

I used to wonder what it would be like to fall out of the second story window. My friend Tony and I pushed the screen out and I got on the windowsill. I slipped and was hanging by the sill. When Tony's mom looked up and saw me, she ran in and dragged me back into the room. I got in a lot of trouble for it, but I don't remember being the least bit frightened.

My dad came and went several times during the next four years and I never knew if he would be home when I awoke each morning. When I was nine years old, I was still very unsettled.

Dad was home, but I never felt like he had much to say to me. One afternoon, I threw a rope over the exposed beam in the carport, tied it off, tied the other end around my neck, and eased off of the brick retaining wall. If I had tied the rope correctly, I would have died. I was slowly choking to death, so I grabbed the beam, removed the rope, and saved myself.

As a teen, I spent years looking for God. I went from church to church, visiting nearly every denomination I could find. I never found any answers that made sense to me. I never found God. Then, one day I felt so alone and so desperate that I again tried to take my own life — this time with pills.

I shudder at the thought of those painful times. I do not regret them, though, for without them I could not be who I am today.

➡

The sound of voices snaps my mind back into the present. I look around feeling dazed, and realize that some of the people are yelling at Johanna and at each other. I stare in amazement as I start hearing the many different voices.

"That's total crap, lady!"

"This is the work of the devil!"

"No, no! It makes sense to me."

"I am not responsible for what happened to me!"

"Wait, I want to hear more!"

"So you're saying that *I* created the car accident that crippled my leg?!"

The ones who are upset are the only ones standing. The rest of us are just sitting there, dumbfounded. A few people carefully get up and sneak off. There, in the midst of the chaos, I see Johanna. She is still sitting next to Jeannie, who resembles a trapped bunny. Johanna is smiling slightly and looking from face to face with total, unconditional love. I feel stunned by what I see. Johanna is completely unmoved and unafraid, looking at everyone as though they are sending her words of love instead of insults.

I want to ask her about Jeannie's healing. I know that whenever I have gone through a deep cleansing and healing and I think I have finally rid myself of the pain, it pops back up time and again. It feels like I have to keep dealing with my painful issues over and over.

Then Johanna's eyes meet mine and their intensity magnetizes me. I cannot move or look away. Then, for no apparent reason, I stand up and walk toward her as though I am hypnotized, stepping through the sea of words and faces. She stands as I approach, and my eyes never leave her eyes — not even to see where I am going. Johanna puts her hands on my shoulders and there is a feeling of power welling up inside of me. Johanna turns to walk away, stops, and says to the crowd, "When you are ready, I will return." Then she turns and walks away. I feel very confused, but I am drawn to follow her.

As I turn to go, I notice Jeannie has crawled away and is huddled under a tree with her friend Roy at her side. I worry for her and wonder if she will be all right. The voices of the crowd fade slowly away as I walk with Johanna. I look to see if anyone else is coming, but they are too caught up in their anger with one another to even notice she is leaving. I wonder where she is going, but I don't say a thing. I just walk away with this remarkable woman.

Chapter 2

"When you have eliminated the impossible, whatever remains, however improbable, must be the truth." Sir Arthur Conan Doyle

I'm roaming the house, unable to settle into my normal routine. The computer hums in the corner of my office, waiting for me to sit down and work, but I can't keep my mind on anything. I try time and again to work, or meditate, or relax, but my mind races with pictures, feelings, and questions. Nothing makes any sense about Johanna – *what am I thinking* – **everything** makes sense about Johanna. In fact, when I'm able to drop the logical side of my mind, I feel a sense of purity and rightness. It's as though Johanna somehow puts everything into perspective just by her very existence.

I plop down on the couch and stare out the open window. The wind is stirring the old pines across the street from my house. The sound of the wind in the trees creates a feeling of restless anticipation within me. The sound reminds me of my experiences even more vividly and a thrill runs through my body like a jolt of electricity. I want to believe with every fiber of my being. I close my eyes to listen to the song the wind and trees create and my mind wanders back to walking with Johanna. I shake my head, as though trying to shake some sense into my memory of yesterday. It couldn't have been real, could it? No. No way. That only happens in dreams and TV... not in real life. Not right in front of my eyes. I shake my head again. I want to discount what I saw, but some deep, inner voice whispers, 'trust what you see.'

The phone rings and I jump. I hear Steve's voice, a good friend I have known for years. I can hear the feather from his hair rustling in my ear. Steve is part Native American and his long hair is white. He has a cute little belly, thick fingers, and piercing hazel eyes. His face is rugged and kind and his manner is gentle. When he smiles, his lips curve up dramatically, and you get a sense that he knows something you don't.

Steve probably knows me better than anyone. His Shaman name is Talking Bear, which really fits his build and his spirit. I decide to tell him about the gathering in the park with Johanna.

"So, what happened after you walked away with her?"

"I don't know, Steve, I really don't."

"What do you mean? How can you not know?"

"I'm just not sure it was real. I mean... I've always wanted to believe that magic exists and that angels and guides are real, but this is way off the scale. I mean, I experienced it and I don't know if I can believe it."

"Tell me, Deb. Trust what you saw."

"What?"

"Trust what you saw. Your spirit will not deceive you."

"Talking Bear, I heard those words in my mind only a few minutes before you called. You're right. I need to quit denying what I saw. It *was* real. There have been too many coincidences to ignore. Here's the rest of the story:

"You know how the park meanders around the lake and if you walk to the left you can go into a wooded area? We walked into the woods and followed a path to the top of the hill. From where we stood, we had the most incredible view of the lake. We sat down and took in the beauty for a long time, without saying a word to each other.

"Then, Johanna looked at me and said that of all the people at the gathering, Jeannie and I displayed the innocence and thirst for truth that it would take to awaken. I asked her what she meant by 'awaken' and she said that every human is more than what we can see and feel. I knew what she was saying, because I believe that way, too. Then she said, 'Allow yourself to clear the cobwebs that filter your view of the truth.'

←

"Everyone has their own story." Johanna begins. "A story is based on past experiences that mold people into who they are today. They create their story when they are young, which is a version of their life experiences and the messages they create from them.

"One experience may be child abuse. They might then build a story around that event that says, 'I'm bad, I'm a loser, I'm powerless.'

"Perhaps they had a healthy childhood, but their first love crushed them horribly. That story could be, 'I'm unlovable, I'm ugly.'

"The important thing to remember is that the story is never true. It is fiction based on feelings and emotions around a specific event from the past. Over time, the story becomes embedded into their consciousness and they start to respond to life from that place. It becomes a truth—a way to live. They have now molded their lives around a false belief about themselves or their environment."

I puzzled over that. "But the actual event is true? So how is that not a true story, then?"

"The event is real. What happened is what happened, but that's not where it ends, is it? This event that happened 30 years ago—in your case, being abused by someone you trusted when you were four years old — is still lived out every day in your beliefs and responses to life's situations. Is it happening now or did it happen long ago? How long did it take you to heal from that event?"

I look at Johanna, amazed that she knows what happened to me when I was four. "I only really let it go last year, after years and years of counseling."

"Exactly! You lived from that event for most of your life, yet it wasn't still happening... it was long ago. But you created a belief around it and carried it with you. And when you felt threatened you would bring it out and use it to compare to your present situation."

"That's true, although I didn't see it that way... I always thought I was using discernment... but in actuality, I was sizing up every man to see if he was safe."

Johanna nods. "And even though you had this discernment, did you make wise choices in men?"

"Not at all. I made some very poor decisions, because I thought that was the best I could do — the most I deserved."

"So your past was running your present and you didn't even know it."

I shake my head at the realization. "Yes," is all I can manage.

➡

"I looked into her eyes, Steve, feeling a little uneasy. Then she smiled and I felt the deepest, most profound unconditional love. I was in love with **the entire world**. It was so immense that I thought I could feel my skin stretching to accommodate it all. Then, she began to glow. It was as though the sun was behind her again, radiating around her body. The light was so intense that I was having trouble looking at her — my eyes were watering from the brightness and I finally had to look away.

"When I opened my eyes again she was gone. I couldn't see her or hear her walking away. It was as though she disappeared without a trace."

"She disappeared. She must have just walked off, right? What are you saying? Were you having a vision?"

"I don't think so. I didn't imagine it, Steve, I know it."

"Wow. That's incredible.... oh, wow. Can I meet her?"

"I don't know where to find her. I have no clue. But Steve, I know I witnessed something miraculous."

"Oh, yeah. You did."

"I don't know whether she's real flesh and blood or an angel or what… I just don't understand. And that logical part of me *needs* to understand it."

"Maybe it's not important that you understand now. Try to let go of your logical side for a little while. Just allow yourself to learn and grow from the experience."

"You're right. Listen, I'm going stir crazy here, so I'm going to take off. I'll call you in the next couple of days, okay?"

"Okay. Love you."

"Love you, too. Bye."

I grab my keys and a sweater and head out the door. I have no idea where I'm going, but I must go. I start the engine and then just sit there, not sure which way to go. Finally, I pull my SUV out of the driveway and get an urge to drive to a friend's house. Jason has some property near the Canadian border that has always seemed very magical to me. It's a two-hour drive, so I gas up and get a snack for the road. It's a good thing my daughter is staying with her father for a few days; otherwise I wouldn't be able to just take off like this.

As I drive toward Jason's, I begin to remember times we spent together — memories of my relationship with Jason. He is tall with rugged good looks and brown hair to his shoulders. His hands are surprisingly gentle and soft considering the way he works in the woods and on his property. His six and a half foot height seemed imposing to strangers, but once you saw the way he laughs you could never be afraid of him. First you see the smile, and then his piercing blue eyes scrunch as he tips his head back and his brown hair sprays over his ears and neck like fine strands of silk and he lets out his belly-deep laugh that shakes his entire body. I laugh out loud at the thought of it.

The year we spent together in my little house in Coeur d'Alene was the most sacred experience of my life. It was in his arms that I discovered how to love for the first time...really love. Not the kind of 'love' I experienced as a molested child.

I had never really understood love or intimacy and I never had a healthy sexual experience...no innocent puppy love or crushes or first love in school. I had crushes on boys, but I was really tainted by my past and there was no real innocence for me.

Once I met Jason, however, I learned to live with more joy and miracles than I had ever thought possible. It was truly a magical time — especially when we would go up to his property for a day or two.

Jason owns 50 acres at the top of a ridge. From the patio that circles his entire log and cedar-sided house is a breathtaking view of

Upper Priest Lake.

I used to have unbelievable meditations there. I remember one time I was meditating and I had a vision that started out as a black spot in my mind. As my consciousness moved away from the spot, I realized the spot was the pupil of an eye. As I progressed back, the eye belonged to a cow, and then I saw scenes of destruction, with people running and screaming. There were explosions of fire coming out of the streets.

I was really shaken by these images, since nothing like it had ever happened to me. I had absolutely no idea what it meant. I found out the next day there had been a terrible earthquake in India and the gas lines below the streets were bursting into flames. That really shook me, because I saw something as it was happening and I didn't know why.

Unfortunately, the relationship didn't last. At the time we were breaking up I believed it was all Jason's fault because he was so controlling. Although there is truth to that—it is also true that I have a very headstrong nature. We were both willing players. I received so many gifts as a result of that relationship. I learned about love, grace, joy, spirituality, and friendship. I learned to honor truth and to stand up for myself. I learned that every person or situation I bring into my life is an opportunity to learn and grow.

Now we are friends. A solid, deep friendship that is a result of our special spiritual connection as well as the history we share.

The closer I get to Jason's, the more excited and restless I feel. I wish he had a phone so I could let him know I'm coming. As I start the climb up the 2-mile dirt road, my heart is pounding with anticipation. All of a sudden, I see Jason's jeep rounding the corner.

"Oh no, he's leaving," I think in dismay. We stop alongside each other and he tells me he's heading to his brother's place in Oregon. My heart sinks, because I know he doesn't like anyone on his property when he's not there. Before I can say a word, he says the strangest thing.

"Look, I don't have to leave for awhile, so I'll come up and visit with you. I have a feeling you're supposed to be here. I had a dream you were coming up today. Now I know why — here you are!" He smiles that great big smile of his and I laugh.

With that, he backs his way up the hill and I follow him. It's always a special treat to spend time with Jason on his property. I get out of my car and we hug for a long time, feeling the love and warmth pass through us.

"Why don't we take a walk? I've wanted to tell you about the plans I have for the property."

I nod enthusiastically. "Plans? That would be great."

We start walking up the hill on a small path worn into the grass and wildflowers by Jason on his countless walks. There are also less obvious paths from the deer that roam his mountain. When we get to the top of the rise, there is a 360-degree view of the lake and surrounding hills and valleys. It is so spectacular that I always feel like I'm seeing it for the first time. I stop and breathe in the air, the view, and the beauty. I start to feel a deep inner joyful peace and I wonder, 'is this what it is to feel God?' I close my eyes and I get an overwhelming feeling of love and well-being. When I open my eyes again, Jason opens his. We smile wordlessly and begin our walk down the backside of the property.

Jason is pointing and talking, proudly explaining all the wonderful plans he has to honor his property. After a few minutes, I begin to feel like I am moving backward even though I am still right behind him. I am having trouble hearing him. His voice is muffled. Suddenly, a flock of crows swoops down right in front of us. Jason acts as if he didn't see them. He keeps walking and talking. I start to interrupt him, but I can't speak. I'm beginning to get a little scared, but I keep walking.

Without warning, an ancient-looking Native American man walks up from behind me and matches my pace. A hawk screams from above. I look from the man to the hawk and back again and he is still there, walking with me. I feel power in this man's presence. Then he begins to speak.

"There isn't much time and you have much to do. Why do you waste energy on the dream?"

I look at Jason, who is still walking on and telling me all about his plan, oblivious to this man and his words. I look back at the man and I am puzzled. "What do you mean? What do I have to do?" I am speaking from my mind to his.

The old man shakes his head slowly, and says, "Don't you remember who you are?"

Jason stops beneath a huge ponderosa pine. Just as he turns around, I begin shaking so hard that I fall to the ground. I see Jason bending towards me, but I am drifting farther and farther away. I sit up and Jason, the old man, and the tree are gone. There is snow on the ground but I don't feel the cold. I see a circle of teepees to my left, and off to one side is a very large teepee. Smoke is billowing out of the top and there are voices coming from inside. I walk over to the large teepee and step inside. There are at least a dozen men sitting around the fire, which casts a golden glow. No one sees me standing there. I watch as they have a heated discussion with one man who appears to be the elder. I look at him closely and realize that it's the man who was walking with me!

Several of the men were talking at once, but I don't understand the language. The old man looks up from the fire and stares directly at me. He nods one time and I feel myself becoming weightless. I begin to swirl like the smoke from the fire as I am being drawn toward this old man. I close my eyes in fear and confusion and when I open them again, I am viewing the scene from the old man's eyes, as though I *am* the old man! Memories of another life and time flood into my consciousness as I see and feel this old man's life.

I feel a *snap!* and I close my eyes tightly against severe dizziness. When I slowly, carefully open my eyes again I am looking up into the ponderosa pine on Jason's property. I sit up and look around. Jason is sitting next to me, and it looks like he is in deep meditation. I wait patiently for him, trying to make sense of what I have just experienced. What does this all mean? Who was that old man and what does he have to do with me? Am I going nuts?

Jason interrupts my thoughts as he says, "So, do you understand now? Do you know who you are?" His eyes are still closed.

"What?" I look at him, feeling baffled. I still feel a little shaky and I close my eyes and try to empty my mind. I sit quietly, trying to make sense of the bizarre experience. Suddenly, a very quiet voice speaks in my mind. All it says is, 'You are One.' I open my eyes and Jason is staring at me.

"Are you okay?" He asks with a warm smile.

"Yeah. What made you ask me if I knew who I was?"

"What?" He looks bewildered.

"You asked me if I knew who I was."

"No I didn't. I was meditating and sending you healing energy. I didn't know what happened to you, but you looked okay, so I waited."

I just gape at him, not knowing what to say. Now *I* feel a little bewildered. "I've got to tell you what just happened." I proceed to tell him of the crows, the old man, my experience, and what he said while he was meditating.

Jason nods slowly. "Sounds like you had a past life experience."

"Past life experience? I don't get it."

"I get the sense that you are supposed to figure this out on your own."

We silently sit there for another twenty minutes and then Jason tells me he has to get on the road. I stand up and we hug.

"Feel free to hang out as long as you want. I'll be gone for two days." He tosses me the key to his house, tells me where to hide it when I leave, and heads back over the hill to his truck.

I sit down and lean against the pine tree, enjoying the breeze. The wind in its branches fills me with a very sweet feeling. I try to make sense of what I saw, but I just feel confused.

"Tell me what you saw, dear one."

I jump three feet and look up to see Johanna standing next to me. "H-how did you get here? I didn't hear you coming." I grab my chest to try and stop my pounding heart.

Johanna chuckles innocently and just keeps staring at me. She sits down in front of me and asks me again. "Tell me what you saw."

I proceed to tell her the whole story and she listens intently. "I think the old man was a medicine man — a shaman. But what does he have to do with me? Why did I see him?"

"What were you feeling as you watched the old man, and later when you were in the village?"

"Nothing, actually. I couldn't feel the cold and there was snow. And when I was walking with the old man, I couldn't hear anything around me but him."

"What I mean is: what were you feeling emotionally?"

I shake my head. "I don't know. Fear I guess."

"Anything else?"

"I don't know what you want me to say, Johanna."

Johanna smiles kindly. "Close your eyes. Think back to your walk with the medicine man. What did you feel?"

"I was afraid at first, then curious."

"What did you feel in the tipi?"

"Confused at first. Then when he looked at me I felt terrified. I couldn't believe he could see me when the others couldn't. But then for a split second, before I came back to the present, there was a moment... a moment of understanding.

"I felt the reason he came to me was to remind me that he and I are the same… I mean, the old man and I must have things in common…." I trail off, lost in thought. Then I quietly (almost to myself) say, "It was like I was seeing that I *am* the old man... or at least, I was." I sit quietly, trying to grasp what I said.

Johanna stands and begins to walk away.

"Wait! Johanna, why are you leaving? Aren't you going to explain any of this to me?"

"I think you understand it just fine. Sit with what you have said. Take time to digest your revelation. I'll be back again when you have need of me."

Then she disappears over the hill. I jump up and run to the top of the hill, but she is gone.

I walk to the house just as the sun is

beginning its descent. I make a bite to eat and take my dinner and a cup of tea out to the deck and watch the sun slowly disappear behind the mountains. There is no logical explanation for Johanna's appearances and disappearances and I really have no experience in this sort of thing, so what am I supposed to think? I'm fairly certain I'm not insane, so now what?

In the morning, I decide to take a walk before leaving and return to the tree where I had the vision and spoke with Johanna. I stand next to the tree, touching it with my hand and get a whiff of a sweet smell. I realize it is coming from the tree and I lean in to get a better whiff. The bark has a wonderful vanilla smell and I breathe it in deeply. I get a warm feeling and give this incredible old ponderosa pine a hug. I reach for a branch above my head and swing a leg over. I climb up so high that I sway with the breeze as I gaze out across the valley. I can even see Lake Pend Oreille from my perch.

Suddenly, I start to shake. The air is warm and I am confused. What is this shaking? What does it mean? My mind starts to spin and I feel the skin on my belly twitching. It feels like it is being stretched taut. My awareness starts to move out of my body, but I feel afraid and the fear pulls me back into my body. I clutch the tree, terrified that I will fall.

"Don't be afraid, little one, you are safe," a

voice whispers. "It is safe to remember."

"Who are you?" I ask in a trembling whisper.

"Remember me and know the answer to your own question."

The voice's whisper is like the wind in the trees. It moves me deeply. I realize that it makes me feel totally safe. I relax again and my consciousness begins to swirl out of my body. It's hard to explain, because I know logically I am in the tree, holding on, yet I also feel myself moving away from the tree in a current of energy. I begin to melt into another consciousness and it feels comfortable. The feeling reminds me of coming home to a toasty house on a cold day. No, it's simpler than that. It's like… coming home.

I'm in a lush green jungle and I can see a primitive village bordering a vast shoreline. I look down at myself and I see that my clothes have changed and my skin is dark. Someone giggles and I spin around to see a young woman. Her skin is dark, too. She seems very familiar. In fact, so does the village. Then, the fog around my brain lifts and I remember. Manatu! Is that you?

The young woman laughs at my facial contortions and says, "Welcome back."

"Manatu, it *is* you!" I run to her and give her a big hug. "What am I doing back here again?

Oh my, I really am here in the Yucatan, aren't I?"

"Well, your consciousness is. Don't forget, we haven't lived here for hundreds of years."

"Why am I here, Manatu, after all this time?"

"You are here to solve a mystery; and when you do you will be changed forever. You will carry the knowledge back to your current life. Come with me."

We walk toward a small hut-like dwelling, remove our sandals, and step inside. It is very simple. An opening for the door, an opening for a window, a bed made of dried plants for the mattress and skins for the bedding. We sit down on skins that cover the dirt floor. As my eyes become accustomed to the hut's dimness, I see bundles of herbs hanging down to dry.

"The mystery is in why you have come back here," Manatu begins. "It is why you have found me again. The mystery surrounds you all the time, but you cannot see it because you have forgotten who you are. You have become the part you play in life instead of the one who plays the part. Do you understand?"

"I think so. Are you saying that I am like an actress who has a role to play, but I have become so engrossed in the role, that I have forgotten I am the actress, not the role?"

"Yes, and this is true of everyone. Some cultures believe that life is actually a dream and that dreams are the true reality. You need to remember who you are so you can awaken from the dream. You are supposed to help others awaken to their higher power, or God essence, but you have forgotten what is true. You became part of the play or part of the dream. We have tried to free you, but the dream is strong and your will to fight has been weakened."

"I don't understand. What do you mean I am supposed to help others? I feel like I can barely help myself most of the time."

"That is the result of living unconsciously for so long. But you have lately begun to question your life and its purpose, haven't you?

"Yes, I have. I sometimes feel like I am just skimming through my life and there are times I feel very empty."

"That is because you have gotten lost. You are here now, which means you are ready to see what lies beneath the life you have accepted as true. You are ready to move into a new realm of living."

"Tell me what I need to do, Manatu. I want to understand. It seems so alien right now to me. But I want to know my purpose and to awaken from the dream.

"Wait, that's exactly what the old man said! Oh.... Manatu, this is what I have wanted for a long time, but I didn't know what any of it meant. I knew there was something else, but I couldn't quite grasp it. It always seemed just out of reach. Help me, please."

"There is only one person who can help you now. It is you. You know this is true. I have intervened in this moment to help you because you have found me again. It is no coincidence that you traveled back to talk with me. You chose to do so because you want to remember. Do you know why you were able to find me again?"

"No, I don't."

"You were able to find me for two reasons. One reason is because my spirit is linked to the land you are visiting. The other is because everything is connected — every person, animal, plant, and rock is part of the essence of Spirit."

"But we haven't existed here for a very long time, Manatu. It's been hundreds of years."

"There is no division of time — there is no then and now. All existence is now." Manatu reaches over and scoops up a handful of sand from the floor. "We are but a grain of sand and God is as vast as the Earth, and the essence of God spans all life that ever was or will be. Now tell me, little sister, what brought you to the land you are visiting today?"

"Well, I am visiting the property because of my friendship with Jason."

"That's the conscious reason. What is the

underlying reason for why you wanted to be there?"

"It seems like the property and I are connected in some way. I sense that I have lived on that piece of property before, if that makes sense."

I proceeded to tell her of my experience with the old shaman. "I feel connected to him, too."

Manatu nods expectantly and touches my face between my eyes. I start to see something in my mind, like a memory I had forgotten. I am struggling with it and Manatu says, "Just relax."

I see myself again... on Jason's property, but long ago. I was a woman — the daughter of a Chief. I was giving birth on that mountain under a ponderosa pine. It was cold and the child was born as the first flakes fell from the sky; I heard a wolf cry at the same moment, so I called her Snow Wolf. I look down at my baby girl and it all seems so familiar. I have a nagging feeling... oh, I... I see her... she's my daughter, Jenny!"

"You have a greater responsibility than to bring truth and light into your own life. You must also bring it to your daughter, Jennifer. She is a great and wise one and she is depending on you to help her awaken to her destiny. You are the only one who can help her. In order to do so, you must first help yourself. No more excuses. Time is growing short."

"What do you mean by that?" The room is

beginning to spin and I feel myself being torn from the moment. No! I don't want to leave! The harder I try to will myself to stay, the faster I spin. I reach for Manatu, but I am too late. There is a loud *crack* and I slam back into my body so hard that I nearly fall out of the tree. I sit there in the pine's branches and weep, feeling lost and alone. How can I possibly do this all alone? I don't know how to wake up. Help me. Please help me. Oh, God, please help me understand.

After spending a good hour crying and feeling sorry for myself, I finally start to crawl down out of the tree. I drop to the ground and hug the ancient pine again, breathing in that sweet aroma of vanilla.

I feel uncertain inside—I know I don't have a clue about how to awaken from the dream that traps every human being—but I know I must try to break through. I must figure it out.

Chapter 3

"Life's full of coinkidinks." Popeye the Sailor.

I start back over the hill toward my car and I begin to pray. "Infinite One," I say aloud as I walk, "please help illuminate my path. I don't know how to begin this new adventure. Where do I begin?"

Suddenly, to my right, there's a movement in the bushes. I stop and look, but can't see what it is. The bushes and I seem to be frozen in time. Then, without warning, there's a hissing grunt and a deer leaps from the bush. He paws the earth and kicks his hind legs, then bolts back into the brush. I am so startled that when a hawk shrieks above me I jump nearly a foot.

"Okay," I say out loud while my heart is pounding wildly, "I suppose that was a sign."

I stand there giving my heart a chance to slow down. Finally, I continue my walk, slowly, and think about what just happened. A deer is normally gentle and wary, but this buck seemed to be challenging me. And the hawk has always been a messenger for me—usually reminding me to be aware of my surroundings and to not take everything at face value.

As I crest the hill, I see a woman on a boulder with her arms raised to the sun. She is clearly a Native woman. Her Raven-black hair moves like silk in the breeze. She is wearing what looks like deerskin. There's a bracelet around her upper arm made of beads, teeth, and feathers. She's chanting quietly. She must sense me, because she stops singing and slowly turns around. Her face is... it... can't be... she... has *my* face! She nods, as though reading my thoughts and then she slowly disappears.

I walk over and I sit down on the rock where I saw the woman. It's warm from the sun. The view from here is marvelous as I take it all in. Who was she? Why did she look so much like me? So now I am imagining myself as a Native American—first the old man and then the woman.

"What does it mean?" I catch myself saying aloud. A breeze comes up and I close my eyes. I've always had a special connection with the wind. I've never really understood it, but sometimes the feeling is almost overwhelming. The only comparison I can think of is the feeling of being in love, only magnified a thousand times.

As I continue to sit on the rock, I get a strange sensation. There's a feeling of energy coming up through me—from the rock. It's warm and vibrant and I am feeling buoyant, as though if I willed it I could fly away. I start to quiver inside and it spreads until my entire body is shaking. I'm scared... I don't know what's happening, but I don't try to stop it. After several minutes the shaking is done and I open my eyes. I am feeling rested and very alert. I start down to the car again, but my senses are heightened and I am aware of everything as I walk. I feel as though I am experiencing everything from three perspectives: the Native woman, the shaman, and mine.

I get into the car and smile at the mountain and my friend's beautiful home. As I drive back toward Coeur d'Alene, I notice everything around me. I also notice that I am much more at peace... with the other drivers, with the traffic, everything. I like this feeling. I begin thinking back to 1991 and the beginning of my spiritual journey.

⬅

I love to meditate or read spiritual books while taking a bath. When I meditate, my mind is not quiet — I seem to enter into a sort of guided meditation, where I interact with advanced souls who assist and guide me whenever I have questions.

The first thing I do once I'm relaxed is to open my crown chakra (I picture it as a water lily opening at the top of my head) and start breathing in the light. I believe that the light is

God's Love. I believe God is expressed on earth as love — love for all.

I draw in the light as I inhale and move it down my body as I exhale. I picture it swirling through my brain, eyes, sinuses, ears…continuing down to my neck. I continue to fill my body with light, down my arms to my fingers, and throughout my chest. I move down the body, lingering wherever I have pain and flooding the area with light.

Any pain or darkness is washed away with the light as it moves through my body and exits through the chakras at the bottom of my feet. When the darker light drains, it is absorbed by the ground, where it is cleansed and converted back to white light.

One of the first books I read about the spiritual path was a book about opening to the higher self and growing spiritually. The farther I got into the book the more focused I became. It was just what I needed to wake up to the truth. The exact thing I need always comes to me right when I am most ready for it, which constantly amazes me. For example, I bought the book and then put it on my bookshelf without beginning to read it. However, a few months later I picked it up and started reading, and it was exactly what I needed to hear.

At the end of each chapter is a meditation. The first chapter's meditation is designed to help me meet my higher self (or God essence). I remember this meditation the most because I didn't expect my higher self to have any particular appearance. In this first meditation I was sitting on a beach watching the waves roll in and out. Someone was approaching and I turned to see who it was. At first, I couldn't make out any features because white light was surrounding the image of my higher self, which was so bright it hurt my eyes. I looked down and a pair of feet came into view. As I looked up a hand reached down to help me. I stood up and saw that my higher self was male and he looked so familiar.

"Who are you?" I asked.

"I am Sananda."

"Sananda? I am not familiar with you."

"I am who you summoned. I am your connection to the realm of light and love— that which you call God."

"What do you mean by my connection? I don't understand."

"Merge with me and understand."

"How do we merge?"

"Open your heart and let me in. Begin by closing your eyes. Now in your mind, find the spot on your chest just above your sternum. This is called your heart chakra. Feel this spot open like a delicate flower. Give yourself permission to accept light through that place. When you feel ready, breathe in the light and love of God through your heart chakra."

I closed my eyes and with my mind I found the spot on my chest he called the heart chakra. When I focused my attention on it and pictured it opening, the spot started to tingle and gently burn. The burning sensation frightened me, but I kept focusing anyway. I breathed deeply and imagined white light entering my chakra and swirling within my entire body. As I exhaled, I felt tension melt away.

I slit my eyes and peeked at Sananda. His head was tilted back and he was absorbing the light of love, too. Then, almost as though it had been previously arranged, light (or energy) from my chakra flowed toward Sananda and the same light flowed from him toward me. The pure white light met and mingled between us and I felt a surge of energy in my chest. I closed my eyes and tipped my head back. The feeling was so incredible. It was like being filled with love, peace, and joy. I breathed deeply which caused the feelings to expand.

"This is what it feels like to be free," Sananda whispered. "This is what you are on your journey to discover. I am your connection to the love and the light; you also have a guide on the physical plane. You will know her as Johanna. Trust her for she is the truth."

"Who?" I ask, but when I open my eyes Sananda is gone.

The memory of that experience still fills me with those feelings of peace, joy, and love. I smile as I drive, remembering so many visits with Sananda in the tub. Each time I meditated with Sananda, I felt more and more anchored in the realization that there's so much more to living than I could comprehend.

Wait! He told me about Johanna over five years ago!

I see a campground coming up on the right and I get a strong intuition to pull in. My logic kicks in and reminds me how tired I am and how I need to get home before dark so I can rest before Jennifer comes home in the morning. Nevertheless, the feeling that I'm supposed to stop is so strong that I pull into the campground. No one is camping and there's light filtering through the trees and dancing on the ground.

I park at the end of the campground and walk into the woods a little ways, listening to the wind sing in the trees. I close my eyes and allow the wind to caress my face. I open them to look around and I see something shimmering in the distance. I squint to try and see more clearly, but

I can't seem to get my eyes to focus on it. Then, the shimmering form starts to congeal and take a shape. I watch, wide-eyed, as the glow diminishes and standing in front of me is Johanna!

Chapter 4

"All the world's a stage and all the men and women merely players." Shakespeare

"Johanna, is that you? Are you real?"

Johanna laughs sweetly and then gently says, "Of course I am real. But I am also a guide. Some call me enlightened. I am One with the Infinite."

"I've had some interesting experiences today, Johanna, but none of them were actually real. So how do I know that you're not just another vision?"

"Come touch me. I am as real as you."

I walk up to her and lightly touch her arm and she laughs that sweet laugh again. I look at her, feeling puzzled.

Johanna motions for me to sit down on a rock beneath a giant Douglas fir, as she lowers herself down to the damp earth. I sit down across from her and wonder why she is sitting on the damp ground in her white dress.

"What makes you think that your experiences were not real?"

"Well, because... they were more like visions or dreams. I only experienced them in my mind."

"Are you sure?"

"Am I sure? I... yes, I think so."

"There are many forms of reality. Just because you can't explain something or it happens in a way that defies what you were taught to believe in, does not make it false. After all of the experiences you've had with Sananda I am surprised you still disbelieve."

"You know about him?"

"Of course, dear one, how can I not know? We are all of the same fabric. All levels of awareness exist simultaneously. There is only one truth and one space. There is only now– this moment.

You think the life you lead is real, but it is actually only a play. You are the one who controls every aspect of it. Is it a happy story, rich in love and abundance? Or is it a tragedy, filled with terror and grief? Who chooses the outcome of life? Every human being chooses moment to moment the course their life takes."

I notice Johanna is using words similar to what my sister, Manatu, used to describe life. "Oh Johanna, I work so hard at changing my life and bettering it, but it never seems to work. I am still struggling with money, although I feel like I follow my leads and take action. It is really frustrating, because I get so tired of the struggle. It's like I'm not truly living—just surviving." My voice cracks as I fight back my tears of frustration. "I deserve to have enough money to live comfortably, but I can't seem to create it no matter what I do. I get so tired of the fight."

Johanna is quiet as she listens. She looks at me with utter compassion. Tears are streaming down my face and I feel miserable. I feel stupid for not getting my life lessons more quickly. I feel like I'm a hopeless cause. How can I deserve to be in the presence of this remarkable woman?

"First of all, receiving is not based on whether or not you deserve it. Every being has the right to the unlimited abundance that life has to offer.

"Secondly, how can you create or 'receive' financial abundance from the universal flow when you believe it's not possible?"

I feel shocked by her statement. "What do you mean? I visualize and do affirmations all the time to create more — and I receive help whenever I really need it."

"Yes," Johanna nods, "you receive small gifts and surprises right on time. You accept these without attaching judgment to them. But then you wish for more, and you pray and visualize, and you don't receive them, right?"

"*That* is the entire problem... that's my frustration! Why can't I create the big things, too?"

"Because you do not really believe it can happen to you. You want it so badly, but deep down you do not think it is possible. So every visualization and affirmation is negated as soon as you finish it.

"Somewhere in your life you accepted the belief that you weren't good enough, smart enough, or talented enough. Then you made a decision: no matter what happens, you can never have the life you want. Maybe other people can have their dreams, but not you."

"But that's not how I feel! I *want* a better life!"

"Of course you do—consciously. But unconsciously you have a belief about yourself."

I puzzle over her words, frowning and thinking back through my life trying to see where I might have thought that way. "I don't understand, Johanna. Will you please help me see it?"

"I would be happy to help you, dear one. Close your eyes and visualize something you want. Make it something big, something you have never been able to create."

I close my eyes and think about the different things I have tried to create in my life. "What I want more than anything is to be a successful published author. I want to make money doing what I love—writing."

"Very good. Now visualize yourself as this author. What does it look like?"

"I am doing a book signing and everyone loves my book."

"Good. Now, how do you feel?"

"I am excited and happy."

"Hold that thought and feeling in your mind. With your awareness, while you are envisioning your future, check your body. Is there anything anywhere that is not happy?"

"Yes. I feel a tightening in my chest."

"Now move your mind from the visualization to the tight feeling. What does it feel like? If you had to give it an emotion, what would it be?"

"It's the feeling I get when I am anxious about something... like paying a bill or wanting to buy something and I can't afford it."

"Exactly!"

Johanna says that so strongly that I snap my eyes open to look at her. She's laughing at my surprise from her outburst, which makes me giggle, too.

"So would you say the anxious feeling is fear-based?"

"Yes."

"The feeling of fear is stronger than your visualization, so it is neutralized."

"Why?"

"Whatever you invest your emotions into is

what will transpire. If you think happy thoughts but fear losing your job, the emotion of fear will overrule the thought and you will probably lose your job. Emotion is the power behind creation. I want you to repeat that back to me."

"Emotion is the power behind creation."

"Again."

"Emotion is the power behind creation."

"Do you understand?"

"Yes..." I say, uncertainly.

"Yes, but..."

"Well, I just remember a few years ago there was a teaching about pictures. We create pictures in our minds of how life is supposed to look and then try to fit life into those pictures. If we achieve the picture then we're in control— we're successful. We've amassed wealth, live in a big house, and drive a new car. It must be true, because everyone is happy when we move in this direction. But we're not happy inside."

I look up, studying Johanna as I continue. "So, the question for me was, how do I create a wealthy, blissful life without mapping myself into the corner of an inaccurate picture?"

"That teaching was speaking to the way people create pictures of what they **think** life is supposed to look like. This was about people getting themselves into trouble by creating a story that they decided was true, and then trying to live up to that story no matter what. The problem with stories is that they are rarely based in truth.

Imagining the life you want to experience isn't about creating a picture. A picture is a snapshot of a life you do not have but think you want. Then, when the picture does not happen, you have proven to yourself once again that life is not fair. Visualization is about taking responsibility for your life as it is now and creating a new future that is fulfilling.

"Also, I hear you saying you have to work, struggle, create, and survive. These are all part of the illusion — the play. If you believe that life is a struggle, and you see your future as hard work and survival, then that will be true for you. The only thing you need to do is be aware of your negative self-talk. Even negative words we say as a joke hold massive power. Your subconscious mind does not know you are joking. It cannot discern humor from truth.

"So you laugh and say, 'I always get lost when I drive that road at night' or 'I wish I could lose these glasses' and your subconscious mind says, 'Okay, if that is what you want.'

My frustration is beginning to grow. "I have been doing this for a very long time. I have used visualization, positive thought, prayer, affirmation, and so on and my life has never improved. I am so frustrated. I am a good person. I deserve a better life."

The dam breaks and I am sobbing in my frustration and confusion. Johanna says nothing, waiting quietly and patiently for my tears to subside. However, they don't subside for many long minutes. Finally, cried out, I sit there looking down and sniffling.

"These questions are the same for nearly every human being. There is a tendency for humans to want to control everything. Most people believe they must be in control or things won't turn out the way they want. The problem with control is that it outlaws magic. A tight rein on a horse provides you with limited choices. Give the horse a looser rein and a more level, pleasant path can be taken while still moving in the same general direction.

"You, dear one, think you are trying to choose abundance. You think you are following intuition with action. Then you despair because it seems as though no matter what you do abundance does not stay with you." I nod as she speaks, surprised by her accurate description of my frustrating dance with life.

"You are using affirmations and following intuition and taking action, but life continues to be a struggle and you wonder why.

"Choose moment by moment the quality of life. Choose your words wisely, because words attract and they have power. Fear often lives in the words we speak. You may say an affirmation 108 times about how you attract money into your life, but then you get a flash of worry and fear because you can't pay the bill that's due tomorrow. That one thought of worry negates all of the affirmations. Why? It is because you fully lived in that one thought of fear. When you repeated the affirmation, did you do it with every emotion you possess? Or did you say it as a broken record, saying the words but feeling nothing? When you thought of the bill that needs paying, did your heart race; did you feel anxiety? When you attach an emotion to a thought you give it power.

"You create your reality moment by moment. You create it by *feeling* what you fear most. If you look closely you will notice a river of fear running right through you. Every time you say 'I can,' a fearful voice whispers, 'Here are all the reasons why I can't.' Fear is powerful because you have made it so by feeling it. Stop. Fear is only as powerful as you allow it to be.

"Trust is the opposite of fear. If you fear, then you are not in trust. Trust yourself. Trust life. Trust love. Trust." Johanna stops speaking for a few moments.

"Surrender is the most difficult to understand," Johanna continues, "because it has been likened to weakness. The weaker surrenders to the stronger. Surrender is just another word for trust. Surrender to the truth because the truth is, you are the essence of light and love, and as such your spirit cannot be hurt or die. Surrender says, 'I have envisioned the life I want and now I release it into the world. The Universe can handle how it will happen. I will concentrate on living each and every moment toward that life.'

"Therefore, the way to create what you want is to feel it with every fiber of your being. Trust your feelings and follow your intuition. Take action when it is appropriate, and do not get discouraged when it does not manifest as quickly as you think it should. When fear rises, you must dismiss it as a false picture and not allow the emotion to course through your body. Surrender to the moment and know you are in the perfect place at the perfect time.

"That sounds wonderful, Johanna, and I have tried to live with those truths. I believe in everything you've just said. I don't know how to make it true for me. I can see how Sarah, down the street, or my best friend, Will, or the stranger in the market can live more in truth and peace, but I can't see it for myself. It's like I am blind to my own inner knowing. I hear the whispering of wisdom inside and I strain to hear, but I can't sift it out from the mind chatter. It's like I want to scream, '**I CAN'T HEAR YOU! SPEAK UP!**' But there's no answer."

Johanna looks at me with understanding. "So, what is the choice you made about hearing your own inner wisdom?"

"What do you mean?" My frustration level rises again in spite of myself. "I make the choice to hear, but it's not obvious to me." I look to Johanna, who just sits there with a *you're not trying* look and I sigh, feeling my own defensiveness. "So… I made the choice to not hear."

"Why?"

"Why? Because if I hear it then I have to listen."

"And?"

"And if I listen, then I have the responsibility to act."

"Why is that a problem?"

"Because sometimes it's scary to make a change. It seems safer to stay with what's known."

"Aaahh. So, the unknown is too threatening sometimes, is that right?"

I nod, feeling foolish because I already know about the unknown and venturing from what's safe in order to find the magic.

"Come. Walk with me through these beautiful woods."

We stand and I turn to walk with Johanna, when I notice there isn't a speck of dirt on her white dress. We head off into the woods, silently. We pick deer paths and clearings and end up on this beautiful ridge overlooking even more ridges. We sit quietly and meditate and when the breeze blows through the trees I feel so connected that I know this is what Oneness must feel like. Johanna finally breaks the hour-long silence. "You lead the way back."

I start down a deer path, but it peters out. "Which way?"

"Choose."

I see a logging road and we take that for three or four minutes, but it's boring, so I start us through the woods. "Is this okay with you?"

"Why do you choose to leave the well beaten path?"

"Because it was boring. There's more of an opportunity to see something neat when I cut through the woods. Besides, it's a more direct way back to the campgrounds."

"So the easiest way is not always the fastest or more direct."

We come to a stop as I survey the way to go. I choose a direction, but it's immediately obvious that it isn't the best way. We turn around and I find a Grouse feather. Johanna looks at my feather. "Was this path a mistake just because you chose not to pursue it?"

"No, but it would've been lot harder if we

had stayed on it. Besides, if we hadn't started on it I wouldn't have found this feather."

Johanna nods. "That's true."

We get back to the campground and sit down. Johanna watches me carefully and then asks, "What have you learned?"

I shrug, not sure what she's getting at.

"Take the experience in the woods and tell me how it coincides with your life's questions."

God, I feel so put on the spot! I wrack my brain trying to get her meaning, then with a sudden **whoosh!** the understanding floods in. I start to talk, full of excitement. "Oh, I see! I choose not to take the easy way or the beaten path in finding my way to truth because I not only want to take the most direct route, but I also want the opportunity for adventure and learning. If I didn't take a wrong turn from time to time, I might not find the special gifts that might be in store, like the feather.

"Did you need to take the wrong turn to see the feather?"

I thought about that for a long time. "No," I begin. "If I had stopped and looked carefully, I might have seen the feather and then I might have realized the path was not the best way to go."

"So, you say this experience is a metaphor for your life. You prefer the most direct route even though it can be more difficult and you find gifts in the adventure along the way. However, if you stop from time to time to survey your surroundings, then you might avoid taking difficult paths that can lead you away from your goal. What other belief are you buying into with your metaphor?"

"I don't understand."

"Repeat what you said to me earlier about not taking the beaten path."

"I said that I don't want to take the beaten path– the way everyone else goes– because I like the adventure."

"Yes. But you also said that you do not like to take the easy way, remember?" I nod, trying to get a glimpse of what she's getting at as she continues. "Does the most direct path have to be the most difficult? Why do you believe that the easy way is less preferred?"

"So you're saying that I can choose to take the most direct path to self-discovery and allow it to be easy?"

Johanna just smiles when I say this. Then, her smile broadens as she begins to dissipate into a mist of white light. "Go in peace, sweet one. Find the path that makes your heart sing. Do not forget to allow others into your world and know they have a world of their own with core beliefs they live by, too. Do not accept their beliefs as your own if they are not in your best interest. Recognize the pangs of fear that stop you."

"Johanna, wait! Don't go yet. I don't know how to make the direct path easy. Please give me some guidance on this, please!" Before I finish the plea, Johanna is gone. "Wait! What do you mean about letting others into my world?" I sit here, confused and alone, wondering if she was even here at all.

Chapter 5

*"Never confuse movement with action." Ernest
Hemingway*

As I drive back toward town, I wonder if I
am hallucinating when I see Johanna.

"If that's true, then I was part of a mass
hallucination at the park," I grumble to myself.
Nothing seems to make any sense to me
anymore. I have always had an open mind, but
when something supernatural actually happens,
I want to disprove it to myself. Why is that?
Why do I doubt the most miraculous
occurrences when I hope to experience them all
along?

I get back to town and my friend, Esther
calls to tell me there's a volleyball game on with
my singles group. I'm not sure if I have the
energy, but I always have a good time with
them.

Esther and I have been friends since we met
at Gonzaga University. It's been about five years
now and I can't imagine not having her as my
friend. Esther is six years older than me. She is a
thin, stunning woman with thick, deep red hair
that's rounded to her shoulders and piercing
blue eyes. She is nearly always smiling and she
has a joyful, loving nature. The few age lines on
her face can't detract from her beauty.

I change and head to the gym to play volleyball with my friends. All the way there I am trying to get all the messages I have received. I want so much to get it all right now…. just get enlightened right now, Deb…. you've been given all the information you need, so just do it! Why is this so hard? No matter how I turn it around in my mind I can't seem to open that golden door that leads to self-awareness. It's like I'm standing there with my hand on the knob, but I don't know how to unlock it so I can step through. Does anyone else ever feel this way?

I run to meet my friends and there's a new guy there. He's cute and we smile a little flirt at each other. I join in one of the games and let myself forget all about the mind aerobics of the last few days.

After the game the new guy, David, asks me to get a bite to eat with him.

"Sure," I reply, flattered. "But I'm a vegetarian, so how about some Chinese?"

"No problem, I love Chinese food."

David is about 5' 10" and his body looks muscular and fit. He has light brown hair like mine, but with a bit of gray around his temples. He is clean-shaven with a square chin and dimples.

David follows me to a great little restaurant and we eat and talk for two hours. I have a feeling I could really grow to like this guy, but I feel a little scared. My life path is so different; could there ever be anyone who resonates with me enough to walk beside me? It's what I want more than anything, but….

"Listen," David interrupts my thoughts, "would you like to go out again? I really want to get to know you better."

"I would like that, too." I feel so nervous, like I'm a teenager again. What's up with this?

"Great! So how about tomorrow night? We could go to dinner and a show."

"Well, that's a little tough. I have an eight-year-old daughter and I don't like to leave her with a sitter on a school night. So how would you feel about coming to dinner at our house and we can watch a movie?"

"That's perfect. I would really like that. I'll bring the movie, okay?"

"Sure. Just make sure it's appropriate for an eight-year-old."

I have been seeing David for three months and he has become a very good friend. He wants to be more than friends, but I just don't feel the same way. David believes we are soul mates. This brings up some interesting feelings for me. Part of me believes in the concept of soul mates, and longs to connect with a man on that level. But part of me believes we each have the potential of being our own soul mate. Once we can grow and heal beyond social conditioning and embrace both our male and female sides, we can be truly whole. But my human side is afraid that being whole is lonely.

There has been a heavy snow so David, Victoria, Diane, Rich, and I head off to the ski slopes one Saturday while Jenny is with her dad. It's an awesome day on the mountain. One minute the sun is out, creating diamonds in the snow. The next minute the fog rolls in and it's like being in a fairyland. And then in another minute or two it begins to lightly snow, which creates another magical scene. Then it starts all over again with some sun and then some fog, and a little snow. I am so filled with wonder and joy that I think I'm going to explode. I have a perma-grin all day long and I am having a *GREAT TIME*.

Each time we get on the ski lift, David and I would take turns talking about ourselves. David tells me all about his work as a surveyor and how he loves his time in the woods. He said, "I could have easily become a hermit and live primitively, but I think I would have missed human contact too much. So I got a job finding old survey markers and updating them. That's where I've been for the last fifteen years."

The more I listen, the more I like him. At one point, as I am listening to him talk, I think, who is this man? I wonder if he's for real.

The rest of the day and the drive home are wonderful. David walks me to the door. "I had a great time, David. Thank you." I smile as we stand in my doorway and then David leans over and kisses me.

"I had a great time, too. I'm really glad we had a chance to be alone together and just talk and laugh."

"Me too. Enjoy your evening with your kids."

"Thanks, I will. Well, see you on Saturday for volleyball." David gives me a hug and then kisses me again and I think my socks are going to fall off. He drives away into the night and I stand there in the doorway, not feeling cold at all. I think I may be leaning toward being more than friends.

Over the next four months, David and I get together once or twice a week. We usually end up talking about life and spirituality until two or three in the morning. It's funny how we can't seem to drag ourselves away from each other. We find excuses to keep talking, just so he doesn't have to leave.

I know I'm in love with David, but I feel as if I'm fighting it. I keep looking for all the reasons why it won't work, yet I find myself loving him more and more each day. One day, out of the blue, David asks me to move into his home in rural Washington State. At first, I am speechless. Then, I think of the timing– my landlord has put my house on the market and I need to move, and my parents are on their way up for a three month visit and I have no place for them to stay. This would solve all my problems! Maybe it's a sign.

David and I discuss building a small home on his property for my folks. It would give us plenty of privacy and I would still have my folks close by. Then if they ever decide to move up from California, they have a place all set up. We look around and finally find a manufactured home for a great price. I put a down payment on it and we arrange to have it moved to David's place. Meanwhile, I start moving my stuff over to his house.

It doesn't occur to me that I am moving in with David way too fast and for all the wrong reasons. Nor do I notice that I haven't meditated or found my quiet place in a very long time — in fact, I haven't been in touch with my inner wisdom in so long that I am neglecting to see just how lost I am feeling. But that doesn't stop me from moving head-on into a situation I probably don't need to experience. It never crosses my mind that I haven't heard from or thought about Johanna in months. I'm losing my way and I have absolutely no idea it's even happening.

David and I start having some difficulties. He's acting really insecure and I don't understand what's going on. He doesn't see that anything is wrong or that his behavior is out of the ordinary. However, he agrees to see a counselor with me to help us through this rough spot. In the meantime, I see a friend of mine who does transformational counseling. She is convinced it will benefit me. As I am talking with Celeste, I feel as though I am coming apart at the seams. It's like I'm about to see the truth and I don't want to. This isn't like me, I think, as Celeste is getting ready to work with me. We do energy work for two hours and at the end of that time I feel I have been cleansed of lifetimes of pain and fear. I feel so refreshed! It's like I have just shed layers and layers of gunk that has kept me from waking up and seeing the dream.

I get the inner guidance that I am not supposed to move in with David, but I feel trapped. Everything is in motion– the manufactured home is being moved onto David's property and I am half moved, too. I feel I am committed to the move, yet every fiber of my being is screaming not to do it. I decide to take the path of least resistance… I move in with David.

Chapter 6

"When first we met we did not guess that Love would prove so hard a master." Robert Bridges

David's place is beautiful– a three-level home on 15 acres of woods with more woods all around his property. His home is north of Spokane, so I am only about an hour's drive from my friends and volleyball. I love taking walks in the morning, listening to the wildlife and breathing in the freshness. This is what I've always wanted! I feel so content. I have the home I've always wanted, and it looks like I even have the loving relationship for which I have been waiting.

David's kids are wonderful, too. His 19 year old daughter, Lisa, is a technology whiz, which gives us a lot to talk about. She is 5'7" with long brown hair and an impish grin. Her green eyes reflect her intelligence and serious nature. She has a slender silhouette and carries herself with elegance.

Sean is 12 years old and built more like his dad: solid. He has brown hair and eyes, freckles, and a great laugh. His eyes dance as though he always knows a secret and isn't going to share.

The manufactured home is delivered and ready for David and me to set up so my folks will have a place to stay when they come up to visit for the summer. One thing after another is going wrong with the manufactured home and it looks like we won't have it ready before they arrive. David is getting really frustrated and I can only do so much to help.

Two weeks after moving in, David has to go to a conference in Seattle and I am flying down to California to help my mom and dad drive up. They don't really need my help, but we always have a wonderful time whenever we travel together. With Jenny staying at her dad's while I am gone, I am footloose and fancy-free for a while.

My relationship with my parents has been rocky at times, particularly when I was a kid. But as the years have passed, I have developed a friendship and love for each of them that transcends childhood memory.

My mother is a kind and compassionate woman. She is now in her seventies, though she looks and acts 15 years younger. Mom is tender and caring to everyone. It's no wonder that so many people consider her their second mom. She tends to be overly controlling, figuring her way is usually the best way. As an adult I can accept mom's nature, but as a kid, I was constantly butting heads with her.

Dad is in his eighties, but he still plays tennis and looks ten to twenty years younger. He is extremely talented. I consider him an electronics genius, but he has the capacity to fix or create anything from woodworking to PC boards. As a kid, dad never spent much time with me, and I grew up feeling like I didn't always have a dad. Now, we spend much more time together. When they are visiting for the summer dad and I play tennis, take walks in the woods, and more.

Both of my parents are extremely intelligent. I often kid them, saying what one of them doesn't know, the other does.

Our annual drive up to the Inland Northwest always includes a stop in Reno for a little gambling. We have never won much, but we have a great time together. We end up taking about a week to get from their home near Palm Springs to David's home near Deer Park.

My parents and I get home before David does, so I put them in the spare bedroom until the manufactured home can be set up. When David finally returns from the conference, it takes us nearly two weeks to get my parents' home livable. David's patience is wearing thin, the folks are feeling guilty for taking David's daughter's room for so long, and I feel like I'm caught in the middle. I take on the role of peacemaker, yet I can't seem to keep anyone happy.

David and I finally get my folks moved into the manufactured home, but I notice that he is still acting bothered. He is getting quieter all the time and he seems really unhappy. I can't seem to get through his defenses. Our fights are escalating and we both feel as if we can't do anything right. David comes home one day and says he doesn't want to live together anymore. I am furious with him for giving up, even though I have been looking at newspapers lately to see what the rental market is like.

Jenny and I move into the spare room at my folks' while looking for a place to live.

My daughter, Jennifer, is a bright, intelligent, amazing, and intense 10 year-old. Sometimes she is wise beyond her years; and sometimes she pushes boundaries so intensely, that she will leave me scratching my head and wondering what just happened.

Surprisingly, that's just a *glimpse* into the inner workings of my complex, beautiful child. On the outside, she is a typical 10 year-old-girl/tomboy with light skin (except in the summer), three rows of freckles across her nose, and blond hair. (As she grows, her hair starts to show increasing honey highlights that fall *literally* like honey.

However, I just noticed yesterday that she has some reddish highlights that seem to flow down her hair like copper threads, glinting in the sun. She will have stunning hair!

Jennifer is adopted and I have noticed that as she grows, she looks more and more like me — except, of course, for her cupid bow lips. My lips are thinner... kind of like chicken lips.

I was very sickly in my mid 20s to early 30s. I was plagued with serious and debilitating pain for two weeks out of every month — from cysts on my ovaries. The worst part was that all I have ever wanted was to be a mother. Rather ironic, even for me.

Once things became life threatening, I knew I had to act. One time in particular happened when I was 22: I had just flown from Washington State down to La Quinta, California (near Palm Springs) to stay with my folks while I was getting over leaving a boyfriend, Simon.

I had been there about a month, when I met Danny. He was my age, cute and funny, with a grin that lit up the night. Danny was just slightly taller than me, and his body was thin and tanned. His hair was black and his brown eyes showed an intelligence and curiosity that intrigued me. We hung out together and took hikes into the canyons at the top of La Quinta cove.

One Friday evening we went out dancing with friends. I felt great and had a fabulous time, other than a fleeting pain in my abdomen. When we got back to my parent's house it was nearly 2:00 a.m. Danny came in with me and we ended up on the couch, kissing and touching.

We slid onto the carpet and made love right there in the living room. Danny's body was muscular and hard and he knew just how to touch me. When he entered me, there was a thrill that shot through my body like electricity.

Just as we climaxed, another feeling shot through my body — pain. My abdomen was on fire with extreme pain. I was doubtful it was gas but I headed to the bathroom anyway as soon as Danny left. Just as I shut the door, there was a searing, jabbing pain in my abdomen that knocked me to my hands and knees. After a few minutes, the pain was so bad that I curled into a ball on the bathroom floor. I had passed out. When I came to, it was 6:30 in the morning and I couldn't stand up.

I literally crawled on my hands and knees to my parents' room and called for help. They jumped up and got me to my bed and then called my doctor, who was stranded in the desert south of Las Vegas. The on-call doctor said it was dehydration from dancing and to give me salt water to drink. The pain subsided enough that afternoon that I felt I was going to be okay. I was weak and dizzy all of Sunday and my belly was really swollen. The pain kept coming and going, so I took it easy on Monday.

When my dad returned from work that evening, he took one look at me and said we were going to the ER *right now*. Apparently, I was as white as the sheet. I wasn't unhappy, since I had this weird headache all afternoon — it was like someone had a hammer and was hitting my head every 5 seconds.
Bang.....bang.....bang.....

I told dad to go have dinner while I waited in the emergency lobby. It was dinnertime when we left. A triage nurse came out to ask me some questions, took one look at me, and disappeared behind the big doors to the ER rooms. Before I had a chance to react to her strange behavior, she reemerged with a wild, white haired older doctor who suddenly halted about six feet in front of me. He spoke to the nurse and she took off through the doors again. As he approached me, I could see a kindly, serious old face. His eyes told me that he was getting tired and how much those eyes had seen. Just as he helped me stand up, the nurse reappeared with a wheelchair.

Once they examined me, there was a flurry of activity, including the dreaded IV. I watched the IV nurse, because she couldn't get into the vein for some reason. She tried all over my arms, and then my legs. After the 12th attempt, the doctor said if she didn't get a vein in the next location, then he was putting it into my jugular vein!

Somehow, bless her, she found one in my right hand after dangling it over the bed and then constricting the veins somehow. She looked at me apologetically when she moved to leave. I nodded with all of the smile I could muster. They wanted to wheel me into the operating room right then and there. I started to get upset because I wanted my folks to help me make that decision. An experienced nurse with dark yellow hair and a white mask snapped down toward my head and stopped 12" from my nose to hers, and spoke rather sternly and loudly.

"Don't you understand? You're dying!"

I just stared at her and thought: how dramatic! "I'm not dying!"

She let out an exasperated sigh and held up my hand. "Do you see how your fingernail bed is white? And look, when I press your nail, there is no change in color."

I shook my head, confused, and she showed

me *her* finger. She pressed and her nail bed went from pink to white. She showed me my nail again and when she pressed, there was no change in color.

"That means you are losing blood internally. Why do you think it was so hard to start an IV or get your blood pressure? It's because you don't have enough blood pumping through your body to keep the veins expanded. Your blood volume is less than half of what it should be"

An aide appeared and said my folks would be arriving in a few minutes, so I asked to wait again.

The doctor looked at me and said, "If they are not here in 10 minutes, we have to proceed or you may not survive."

I nodded, feeling *so* confused. I mean, after all, how can I be dying?

My folks arrived and were apprised of the situation. They came over and said I needed the surgery right away. When I looked at their faces, I saw how real their fear was.

I barely survived the cyst that exploded and tore my ovary open.

The cysts kept growing to differing sizes over the next few years, some of which were life threatening.

I married my first husband, Al when I was

25 years old and in 7 years I had 5 major surgeries to remove cysts. All the cysts and surgeries caused other painful problems, too: adhesions and endometriosis.

Al was about 5'9" with a well-built, tanned body from working outside most of his life. He had a kind face and people liked him instantly when they met him. His brown hair was always cut neatly and his hazel eyes seemed to laugh when he was happy.

Al may not be as tall as some men, but he is a giant inside. He is the most honorable and honest man I have ever known. Add to that someone who likes to smile and has a great sense of humor. I always found him attractive...especially the laugh lines he gained from being happy — happy just because.

I couldn't get pregnant with all the problems, which tore my heart apart every month…I wanted to be a mom. In the summer of 1986, we started adoption classes with the county. We were foster parents for infants and toddlers, so we were known by most of the social workers. We graduated in October, and in February I had a hysterectomy and had it all removed. I cried every day for over two weeks.

In May, I decided being a foster parent was too painful…they always went away again. So we gave away most of our baby things to one of Al's employees, since he and his wife were having their first child. The only things they didn't need were the crib and car seat. We put those in the garage.

That July we were called by a social worker I knew and asked if I would take a newborn for a day or two. I explained I had just given everything away, bottles, blankets, and furniture. She sounded desperate, so I said, "Okay, I will buy a bottle and a couple of things I will need. Just for a day or two, right Tracy? It's so painful when they leave."

She assured me that was all and said she would call in the morning to verify that the child needed a temporary home.

The next morning, Tracy called and said, "I wasn't completely honest with you, Deb. I just wanted to make sure everything was in place before I promised anything. She was born this morning and she is yours if you want her."

I dropped the phone receiver in shock and then scrambled to pick it up and breathlessly said, "YES!"

That's how Jennifer came into my life.

➡

We have been at the folks' mobile for about two days when David changes his mind and wants me to stay. He doesn't seem to know what he wants and neither do I. Everyone is on edge — the kids feel uncertain about their future and my folks think our problems are because they are visiting. Everyone wants to take the blame.

We talk about commitment and choosing to see this relationship through. We decide to give our commitment a specific length of time — one year. One year, with a no-exit clause to keep us from running away from each other. We both agree to it. Summer is nearly over and my folks are heading to Seattle to visit one of my brothers. The last two months have been a challenge, but with the no-exit agreement I feel we have a good chance to turn this relationship around.

The kids go back to school in a week, and Jenny is looking forward to starting her new school. David and his kids go on an overnight camping trip before his daughter goes back to college, and I stay home with Jenny so they can have some bonding time. David, Lisa, and Sean come home the next day and the kids are radiant. I can tell they had a good time. Jenny and Sean start playing in the yard as I go out to the garage to see David. He looks miserable and my heart skips a beat, feeling afraid that he is unhappy again.

He says, "I don't know if I can do this commitment, Deb." I flip out and storm to the house. The kids stop playing in their tracks as I am yelling at David all the way to the house.

"**So much for commitment**," I scream. "**That's just fine, because I'm leaving!**" I storm up the stairs and start packing a bag. I tell Jennifer to pack a bag, too. We are going to town to find a place to live. She starts crying and Sean gets really quiet.

David follows me to the house and up to the bedroom. "Leave me alone," I seethe.

"C'mon, Deb, let's talk about this."

"I'm through talking to you." I say as I grab my bag and start throwing things into it.

He keeps trying to touch me and talk to me, but I am too angry to let him in. Finally, I turn to him with one of my shoes in my hand and shake it at him, saying, "I'm warning you, leave me **alone!**"

He waves his hands in the air and backs off, saying, "Okay, okay. I'll leave you alone." David leaves the room and I finish packing my stuff. I throw Jenny's and my things into the manufactured home and then head to Coeur d'Alene to buy a paper and see friends.

I spend a couple of days in Coeur d'Alene, looking at places that I found in the paper. Finally, with only a couple of days before school starts, I find a neat condo in a secluded little community called Twin Lakes about twenty minutes from the city. I am close to the lake and the condos are nestled in some of the tallest Ponderosa Pines I have ever seen. I rent a moving van and move out of David's house with the help of the kids.

Jenny and I get settled just in time for school, and my folks come back and stay with us for a couple of weeks to make sure I'm okay. I feel such a sense of relief that I don't even notice that I haven't grieved about the break up with David. My anger is keeping me from feeling sad, and I'm not allowing myself to see it.

Chapter 7

"On this narrow planet, we have only the choice between two unknown worlds. One of them tempts us—ah! what a dream, to live in that!—the other stifles us at the first breath." Colette

Al stops by to see if we are okay and to commiserate with me. We visit for about an hour over some hot coffee and then he stands to leave. We hug briefly and he looks into my eyes. I know Al is still in love with me, I only wish I could return his feelings. This is all very reminiscent of our third attempt to get back together.

←

I found a mobile home and five acres north of Spokane in the spring of 1991 and made a small down payment to hold it until the spring semester at Gonzaga was out. I only had four weeks before the summer semester started, so I started packing every chance I had.

I went up to the property one evening with about a dozen seedlings of Spruce, Pine, Fir, and Cedar to replace the back hoe's work. That was the first time I ever met a tick. As I'm driving home, I find myself pulling several out of my hair and throwing them out the car window with a loud, "Ewwwwwwww!"

Al and I had been talking and dating, so we tried yet again to make a go of our relationship. He started to help with the packing and my folks came up for their annual visit and helped, too.

Once we got everything moved over to the property my folks went to see my brother in Portland. Al and I got moved in and we had Jennifer's fourth birthday in the trailer. It was very hot weather for July and we had no air conditioner. Jenn's cheeks were beet red and once we had her little party and the cake finished, we all went outside under the trees to cool off.

My folks returned two weeks later and were fortunate to follow a cooling trend that took us from the mid-90s on Jenn's birthday to the mid-70s one week later. One night, I was awakened around 12:30 to a strange glow coming from the night sky. I looked out and could not believe my eyes. I woke everyone and we went outside to look at it more closely. It was like there was a river of white light flowing across the sky, moving and undulating.

We found out the next morning that what we saw was the Aurora Borealis. I have seen many pictures of the Northern Lights, but none quite like the one we saw last night.

Even though there were no real problems, it was clear to me that it wasn't going to work with Al. He moved out around the middle of September, about the same time my folks headed back to California.

There is only one reason we are not still married — I loved him deeply as my best friend and confidante, but I didn't have the passion of a wife...not for lack of trying. I didn't understand that there is a difference between the enduring brother/best friend/trusted confidante love and the passionate love of couples who are both moved by that love.

It was the middle of the night when I awoke from a strange dream. It took a long time to go back to sleep and in the morning I had a nagging feeling that something was wrong. This happened every morning since, but I couldn't figure out what it was about. As each week passed, the feeling got stronger and more insistent. It was the end of September and the nagging feeling would no longer pass. In fact, there were words with the discomfort: you need to move. I dismissed it, because I finally had a place of my own in the woods and out of the city.

Unfortunately, the words became louder and more insistent every day, until I awoke to the voice literally screaming in my head the first

week of October: YOU NEED TO MOVE…
NOW!

I felt very confused but the next day I went into town, got a paper and started looking at rentals. Spokane is an interesting place… it still has an eclectic hometown feel even though it is a large city. It's a lot like the feel I get in Portland, just on a smaller scale (Spokane is a little less than half of Portland's size). Spokane's streets are another matter, however. You can never assume a road goes through, because more likely than not, there is a large gap with neighborhoods separating it at some point.

I looked at quite a few houses until I found a sweet turn of the century home in East Spokane. It was being rented out by a retired marine corps general, Mr. Wes Wilmet. He looked and sounded like a gruff, tough guy, but he was actually kind beneath the bravado.

I had decided to take the place and met him to sign the papers and give him a deposit. When I arrived, he looked shaken. His large barrel-chested body was slumped slightly and he was a bit pale. His ears seemed to be pricked beneath his silver hair. Mr. Wilmet grabbed me by the arm and walked me outside onto the porch.

"Look," he said seriously, "I am a strong, brave man who has seen a lot during my life; but I have to confess something I don't even believe in."

I was truly surprised and curious about his statement. "What is it, Mr. Wilmet?"

"I have to tell you before you move in...it...wouldn't be fair or safe if I didn't. I am the last person on this earth to believe in the supernatural or ghosts, Mrs. Christy, but something is odd about this house.

"A friend and I were changing out the old dining room chandelier for a more updated one. When we were done, I double-checked the screws to make sure they were tight. As we were leaving, my friend checked it again and it was solid.

"We went to dinner before tackling the bathroom and when we returned, the light fixture had crashed onto the floor and my watch dog was cowering in the corner of the kitchen. We checked everything thoroughly; nothing was broken, the ceiling didn't give way, the screws were not stripped...it was as though someone unscrewed it and let it fall.

"Mrs. Christy, the doors were all locked from the inside and the deadbolt was used on the front door. No one was in the house or my dog would have *him* cornered and not be acting like this," he waved the air as though pointing to the corner and the dog. I think the house... might... be.... haunted."

I smiled at the aging yet dynamic man when he grimaced at the end, as though I might laugh in his face.

"I'm fairly intuitive, Mr. Wilmet. Let me walk through the house with my daughter and I will let you know what I think."

He shook his head as he glanced at the car where my daughter was waiting.

"It's ok. We will be safe. If not, we will leave right away, I promise."

I went to the car and asked her to walk through it with me. We walked in, hand-in-hand, and started to look around.

My four year old daughter pursed her lips at me in the kitchen and said, "Something feels different here."

"Well, Mr. Wilmet thinks it might have a ghost."

She gave a "that makes sense" nod and kept looking around on her own. I checked out the places important to me, like the kitchen, bathroom, and my bedroom. She checked out the places important to her, like where she will sleep and how big is the yard.

As I walked through the rooms and look around, I got a sense of safety and warmth from the house. It's as though the house wanted us to live there. Not a ghost, but a benevolent home.

Jennifer ran up to me and said, "Mom, we should live here. I think we're supposed to."

"Really? Why do you say that?"

She shrugged and said as she skipped out, "I dunno. It feels good here."

I walked out behind my skipping child and told Mr. Wilmet we would take the house.

We were all moved in by October 10th, but the boxes would take longer since midterms were around the corner and I needed to study every chance I got.

On October 16th, I got home from school around 3:00 and the television was alive with reports of fires all over Spokane and neighboring counties. I could see the haze and smoke in the distance when I stepped outside, mostly to the west and north of me. By the time I picked up Jennifer from her Charter School at 4:00, the smoke was thicker and rose high into the sky. I checked the news every couple of hours to make sure we were not in the way.

The next morning, the news was all about the fires. They were calling it a firestorm. There was no danger for the city of Spokane, so we went to school as usual. That evening, the firestorm had a perimeter of over 100 miles. It was the worst fire in Spokane's history since the great fire of 1889.

They showed the areas that were devastated and the locations that were being evacuated because of the threat. My trailer and five acres were right in the path of the wall of fire! I immediately called my old neighbors to see if anyone needed a place to stay, but found out they had all gotten out and were staying in town.

I suddenly thought about that insistent voice in my head. So *that's* why we had to move. I took a moment and thanked those voices for guiding me, even when I didn't want to listen.

I took a drive out there a month later to see the damage, and everything was a charred mess. The trees, the mobile homes, and the landlord's house were gone.

➡️

Jennifer and I go to Sarah's house, where we meditate with a group of friends on Thursday evenings. We meditate while Jennifer and Sarah's son, Josh are playing in another room. Jennifer tiptoes in and sits with me. When we finish meditating she slips onto my lap as we begin our discussions.

Brenda is explaining her frustration with staying in the Oneness, which is the recognition that we are all connected to each other, that we are all part of the same source of energy, bliss, and love. She realizes that her separation from source comes from fear, and that fear is the illusion that separates from the essence of God.

Brenda says her life seems to pull her every

which way. "I feel like I finally reach a deep state of love, and then something happens to cause a crisis and I am snapped back to the reality that life happens and I am stuck here to keep facing the crap."

Many of us nod in understanding. It seems we all have the experience of wanting to recognize and live in the Oneness, but no one seems to know how to stay there.

Suddenly, Jennifer pops up out of my lap and turns to face us. Before I can ask her what she's doing, she starts to talk. We all stare at her, dumbfounded, because she is talking with a knowing no 10 year old should have.

"Don't you get it?" Jennifer asks. "You are all here for one reason: to remember what you have forgotten. You have all forgotten that you **are** the Oneness. You are not here to learn how to love one another. You are here to remember that you **are** the love. You are **not** the bodies you occupy. Your bodies are the vehicles you use to navigate the physical plane of existence. You are infinite beings who have chosen to come to this place of physicality.

"It all comes down to choice. You chose this life and you create it with every choice you make. You are free to choose the kind of life you lead. You are free to choose the crises and chaos or the love and bliss. You are unwittingly creating every experience and you don't even know it!

"Many religions talk of Heaven and Hell as places you go to when you die—the truth is you create your own Heaven and your own Hell right here on Earth. Is your life mostly heavenly or mostly hellish?

"You all want the answers given to you… no one wants to gain the knowledge through understanding and growth. Therefore, I give to you this answer: *You* are the creator of your life. *You* control the action, the drama, the humor, the happiness, and the grief. You receive signals every day that let you know if you are following the path of the heart.

"Are you miserable? You are not on the path to your highest potential. Are you suffering in some way emotionally or physically? You are struggling with the illusion and not following the path of the heart.

"You are here to remember who you are. You are here because you want to wake up to your true, infinite self."

Then she gets a funny, 'what are you staring at' look on her face and then runs into the other room to play with Josh.

I open my eyes and sit up, shocked that I'm alone and in the dark.

"It was all a dream," I say aloud in amazement. I quickly grab my dream journal and write the dream down, word for word. I lie back down and marvel at having such a vivid dream about meditating with my friends, especially since I will be at Sarah's to meditate tomorrow night. Just as I am about to fall back asleep, I could swear I heard Johanna giggle.

"Johanna," I think sleepily. "It's been so long."

I arrive at Sarah's house a little early, so I can share my dream with her.

"Did you bring the dream journal with you?"

"Yes, as a matter of fact, I did."

"Perhaps you can share it with the group after our meditation."

"I would love to share it."

After our meditation, I share my dream. Brenda's eyes widen as I read it, and when I finish, she explains that she had that exact frustration and was planning to talk it over with the group.

We all look to one another for an answer, feeling very confused. "I guess this just proves that we really are all one, that we all share the same energy and God source," I affirm.

The words remind me of the way Johanna speaks and I remember hearing her giggle as I fell back asleep.

"You know," I start, "there is a lot of truth to the words in the dream. It's no accident that I had the dream the night before I was to come here to meditate. I think it's time we look honestly at how we each promote the illusion of fear and separation."

"Brenda, you said in the dream that every time you feel connected to the oneness a crisis takes you away from that place. Is that accurate?" Brenda nods and I continue, "Why do you think that you create a crisis to take you from that place of peace? What core belief do you have that switches on whenever you get to a place of bliss?"

Brenda bites her lip as she thinks about my question. I look around and everyone seems lost in his or her own thoughts. I begin to search my mind for my own unproductive core beliefs. A strange feeling interrupts my thoughts. It is as though there is someone whispering in my ear. I tell Brenda to allow herself to *feel* the belief with all of her physical and emotional ability. "Now, follow that belief back to where it lives. Follow it all the way back to its beginning and see the face of the lie that created it."

Suddenly, Brenda exclaims, "I know! Whenever I would be happy as a kid, my dad would tell me not to be so rambunctious—he would always tell me to calm down and be a lady. My mom would always talk to me about how I shouldn't get my hopes up in life. She said that every time she and dad would get a little money ahead, something would break down and have to be replaced, or one of us would get hurt or sick. They pounded into me that everything in life is like a punishment and there is no reward for living a good life and being a good person."

"So, how do you feel about that belief system?" I ask. "Does it work for you?"

"No! I hate it. It's like I took on the belief by default, because I didn't have a belief of my own."

"So what do you think of that core belief now?" asks Sarah.

"I think it stinks. It doesn't work for me. I think I had better make a decision about what I perceive as the truth so I can put the old belief system out of commission."

Tim asks, "How will you do that?"

"I honestly don't know."

Donna offers a suggestion: "What about affirmations to reprogram your subconscious mind with the new information?"

Then Vickie adds, "Yeah, like erasing the old tape that no longer fits and replacing it with a new recording."

"Also, something I just learned," I start, "is that we create undesired outcomes by attaching emotions to our fears. So, if you feel at peace with everything and then a thought of lack comes into your mind, you give the thought power by experiencing the emotion tied to it."

Brenda nods. "That makes sense. I hear myself saying things like 'it's hard' to do this or that. I know better than that. It's only as hard as I make it. I am going to really try and change."

"Try?" Bill asks. "Don't try. Make a choice: either change or don't." We all nod in agreement.

Brenda stands and thrusts her right arm up and says, "You're right. I choose change." Then she bows dramatically. We all laugh and applaud.

We spend the rest of the evening talking about our new commitments to realize all of the ways in which we unconsciously sabotage ourselves with old core beliefs that we acquired by default, usually during our childhood.

I spend the half hour drive back home thinking about the meditation and discussion. Jennifer is asleep in the passenger seat. I get home, pour Jennifer into bed, and then call Esther to tell her all about the dream and the meditation.

"What do you make of it all?" She asked.

"I don't know exactly. I realize that my subconscious doesn't know when I'm serious or joking—that sayings like 'it's hard for me,' or 'we can't afford it,' or 'I can't' is recorded into my subconscious and then it provides those outcomes for me.

"I also know that I am more than I seem. I have had some messages delivered to me lately and I am having a hard time believing it all."

"Why?" Esther retorted. "You have been searching for truth and growth ever since we first met seven years ago."

"I know, but I get a real sense that I'm fighting it. It feels too scary to step out on that limb. It means that things will be different... I will have to change everything about me. I will have to always be on my guard and watch everything I say and do."

"That's your fear—that's not necessarily reality."

"You're right. It's my fear. I'm afraid that if I accept everything I have been told in the last few days that I will have to work too hard to change. It's easier to stay where I am than to think about changing and moving into the unknown."

"**That's** what you need to look at—you're fear. Nothing else is true unless you create it through your fear. Don't forget… we bring about what we think about."

After talking with Esther I realize that she is right. I can create any reality I want just by choosing whether to dwell on what I fear or not. I can imagine any life experience, but what I will receive is what I fear the most, because that's the strongest emotion.

This is getting so complicated. All I want is to quietly grow and not create anything bad and have all of my needs and desires fulfilled. 'Gee, Deb' I chide myself, 'don't we all.'

Chapter 8

"The will is never free—it is always attached to an object, a purpose. It is simply the engine in the car—it can't steer." Joyce Cary

I decide to take a bath to relax my body and my mind. As I sink down into the hot water and fragrant bubbles, I let out a loud sigh and realize how tense I've been lately. Jennifer is in bed and I know this is a perfect opportunity to meditate. It's funny how I have my best meditations in the tub. I close my eyes and empty my mind. I hum a mantra I learned from enlightened teachers in Colorado.

Suddenly, I hear a giggle. I'm sure Jennifer is out of bed as I open my eyes and look around. No one is there. I quietly call out to her.

"Jenn? Are you up?"

No response. Hmmm, I must have imagined it. I close my eyes again and return to that quiet space. There it is again—that giggle!

I allow myself to relax in spite of my uneasy feeling. Johanna's face comes to my mind and I can feel myself smile. There is always such a feeling of love when I think of her. I have a wonderful meditation—in fact, it's the first time that I really feel as though I have been able to empty my mind and have no thoughts.

Once I'm out of the tub I straighten up the

house a bit, and then I slip into bed, falling asleep easily. Just before waking, I have a dream:

I was in David's house and I was taking his daughter Lisa up and down on a secret elevator I had found. It was small-- only about three or four feet square.

Then time had passed, like a year, and I was sitting at the table with Lisa and Sean. Sean was trying to do math homework. The teacher wrote the math problem on the leaves of plants. He was trying to do the math on a marigold leaf, and when Lisa and I tried to help him, he got defensive and acted like we didn't know what we were talking about.

Then, I took Sean on the secret elevator. When we got down to the basement, I could see David outside working on the house. It was sunny and warm and he had his shirt off. The stuff in the basement was neat and arranged, but there was a heavy layer of dust all over everything. The windows were letting in light.

We went back up and got into David's work truck. We passed Lisa and waved as she got into a convertible with a bunch of her friends. Sean pulled out a tape by a group called Stones and Bones and was planning to play it. I was driving and Sean looked down and noticed I had on moccasins. I told him they were the ones from the elevator. They had a hole and I could see my toes. I thought about how I should stitch them back up.

Sean saw something beautiful up ahead (I think they were whales) and I drove toward the dirt road that went along the water. I was about to turn on the dirt road, remembering it was the one I was on the day before when a police car was behind me, but didn't stop me.

Suddenly, I realized that I couldn't make the turn without falling off the cliff and into the water below. I slammed on the brakes, and we were on a steep angle facing the long drop. I knew that if we even leaned forward the momentum would take us over the edge to our deaths.

I didn't know how I was going to back us up using the clutch pedal without creating a slight forward motion, which was all it would take to make us fall. I leaned back in the seat and the car rolled back off the ledge. I was really relieved, but Sean was just looking at me, like I was over-reacting.

I lay in bed, trying to make sense of the dream. I know it's significant, because I always remember my dreams when my higher self is trying to get a message to me. I write down the dream and then begin analyzing it. My dreams have always intrigued me, because if I don't interpret one correctly, then I will continue having dreams that are similar until I figure out the message and then they stop. I pull out my dream book to assist me in the interpretation.

I decide that the elevator and basement symbolizes moving to my subconscious. A teacher in my dreams usually refers to my spiritual guide or 'higher self.' The 'problem' is written on a marigold leaf. I use an infusion of marigold blossoms and leaves for eye infections, so the problem could be that I need to be willing to see what's true and pay attention to things that cause me to get defensive and shut down. I probably even doubt the messages from my own inner knowing. My conscious mind may be trying to understand my problems analytically, instead of intuitively. When my superconscious (or higher self) tries to speak truth, the conscious mind gets defensive and angry.

When I take my doubting side down to my subconscious levels, I see my spiritual foundation appears neat and organized, but I tend to neglect it or ignore it. However, there is light (understanding) streaming in. David is the emotional physical fear that I have created. The truth is bared and I have all the facts I need to see beneath the fear.

I continuously work at recognizing the beauty in life. I like the fact that my spiritual growth provides insights of harmony, foundations of truth, and the idea of being changeless, but my subconscious mind is hard-driven, with no tender loving care. It sees life as being a struggle, and doesn't understand why I try to change.

When I get too close to awakening to beauty and truth, I slam on the brakes because I am afraid of the fall. My social conditioning kicks in and tells me how spiritual awakening is a lie: life is a struggle and then you die. Could this be a warning that I'm heading for a fall?

I need to sew up any holes in my respect for myself and others — walk softly, peacefully, yet stand tall. Look at how the details and little things in life are handled. In creating my path to truth, I need to watch for feeling guilty or being harsh and judgmental with myself. Let go of feelings of right and wrong.

I close my eyes to let it all sink in. It feels like an accurate interpretation, but there is something else tugging at me. There's more, but I can't quite grasp it. I see an image of Johanna in my mind's eye. I breathe deeply and Johanna appears more real.

"You have a question for me," she states.

I look at her, wondering what she means. "I have a question?"

"Yes. Think about it for a moment."

Then, I remember a question that I had some time back but didn't know whom to ask. "What is the purpose of the will?"

"It is a gift of spirit. It is what you would call a foundation, in which to build all other forms of thought that you would choose. Do not allow the will to control you, or your thoughts, or your human emotions, for then it changes from a gift to a prison. You can (and you do) choose how you intend to use the will. By itself, it is raw power, raw energy. It is untamed. Unite the will with love from the heart and wisdom from the mind and you will have a positive force to fulfill your needs, wants, and choices. You will be enabled to better serve others as well when your will is in balance.

"Open your heart and your mind and know the truth, for what is important is not whether you desire a vehicle or whether you desire monetary sustenance. It is how you limit the possibilities in your conscious and subconscious mind. Examine these beliefs."

"How does desiring things relate to the will?"

"You think you can use 'will power' to bring things you want into your life. While this is true, will power that is not grounded in truth and wisdom has more of an opportunity to succeed in unforeseen ways. In ways you may not want to happen.

"There was a man who wished to have a large sum of money. He did not care how he got it, just as long as he got it. So, he wished for the money, pictured having the money, literally tried to will it into being. He didn't ground his desire in truth or love. He just wanted the money. So one night he was driving down the highway and a deer stepped onto the road in front of a car going the opposite direction. That car swerved to miss the deer and hit the man nearly head-on. The man lost his leg and one of the passengers in the other car died. The man received a very large sum of money from the other driver's insurance company."

"That's a terrible story, Johanna!"

"That is a true story that illustrates what can happen if a desire is not tempered with love and truth. In truth, he didn't want to lose a leg. He didn't want someone else to die to get the money. But he told himself (his will) that he did not care how he got it.

"There is another story like this about someone who did not use love or wisdom in the wish for money and she received it through a relative passing away and leaving her money. She loved this person and it was not how she wanted to receive.

"Most of the time people use their will out of fear, not love. They are afraid that if the money doesn't come, something terrible will happen. They might lose their house, car, or family. But the fear of loss is a powerful emotion and it is like a magnet for all you do not want."

"So how do we get what we want without creating what we don't want? What do you mean by creating with love and wisdom?"

"It is paramount to understand the emotion that is present when you work on attracting what you want. You must be very clear, because any desire that is not based in love can have deleterious effects."

"Can you give me an example of creating with love?"

"Yes. Let us say that you want to create receiving a sum of money. First of all, do not attach yourself to a specific dollar amount. For example, you may want $10,000 to pay your bills and give you a buffer while you find work that matches your passion."

I nod. "That sounds about right."

"There are three things you must do to prepare yourself to receive. First, you must ground yourself in love. Anything desired from feelings of desperation or fear will either not materialize at all or will come in ways that cause pain.

"Second, don't constrain your possibility to create what you want. Instead of saying 'I want $10,000' say 'I want at least $10,000' or 'I want more than $10,000.'

"Third, you must act as though you have

already received. Prepare for what you want. In the example of the $10,000 you can sit down, organize your bills, and create a tally of all the balances so you know how much money you will need. Picture yourself joyfully paying off each bill. Really feel the joy and relief. Decide how much you will put into savings. Plan to keep some of it for yourself and shop around for what you want."

"I love that! Those are great ideas — and it brings me to one of the real confusions I have about attracting what I want. I have heard the suggestion about acting like you've already received. I never understood how do you do that. If I don't have enough to pay a bill, then I don't have enough. If I see something I want to buy and I don't have the money, how do I afford it?"

"I see. The adult mind forgets how to make believe. Children make believe all the time. They daydream, they wish, they play at what they want. If you are looking at your bills and you are feeling anxious, you are not looking at what you want to have but what you *do not* have. You do not want to have these bills and you are sick of not having enough money. Then you wonder why you have a headache. You are literally making yourself sick over not having enough.

"As soon as you feel yourself saying you do not have enough, change the feeling. Change your words and change your emotion about it. Bless the bills and send them love. After all, they provided you with something you needed. Be happy and grateful that you have the opportunity to pay these bills. As soon as you feel tightness in your chest or anxiety about something, stop. Learn to recognize that feeling and then change it. That feeling is what keeps you from having what you want.

"As far as seeing something you want, instead of saying to yourself, 'I cannot afford that,' say 'I am looking forward to buying this!' and then picture what buying it and owning it will look and *feel* like. Make space for it in your home or wherever it will live. The reason this is so important, is because you are moving the object from wanting it to having it. If you want something, does that not mean you do not have it yet? Can you see how that creates the attitude of lack? You attract what holds the most emotion for you, so lack and fear are very strong emotions."

"Oh, I get it! That makes so much sense."

"Release the fear that is connected to money. Stop being afraid you won't have enough. Separate truth from fear and you will manifest what you want. Trust that you always have what you need *before* you need it. Only you can manifest your abundance through spirit and only you can deny it of yourself. You choose moment to moment what you believe."

"How do I reprogram my subconscious?" I ask next. "How can I change the basic belief structure in my mind when it is usually so invisible to me?"

"By believing, envisioning, and affirming with emotion. By releasing the fear, and by embracing love. You create abundance by choosing what is real for you and following truth.

"People create abundance every day... it can be an abundance of pain, it can be an abundance of horror, it can be an abundance of truth, and it can be an abundance of joy. Yes, it can even be an abundance of money. When you choose to create your abundance with truth, with the outcome toward service or helping others, with love and compassion, then you create an abundance that is fulfilling and forward moving."

The telephone rings and I nearly jump out of my skin. The conversation with Johanna was so real, that I forgot I was still lying in bed! I grab the phone and sit up against the pillows. I hear my Cousin Karen's voice at the other end.

Karen is in her 40s but you would never know it. She is very thin and she has long honey-colored hair with strawberry blonde highlights. Her blue eyes are intense and you can feel her piercing your soul with her power and her love.

Karen has been in Scotland for several months. She originally went there on vacation, but loved it and wanted to stay longer. She started looking for ways to make some money and found an incredible opportunity in Dundee. She started assisting a professor in the Energy Department at the University of Dundee. Karen is helping her compile data on energy conservation. Karen has this amazing ability to create anything she wants. I have never known anyone who could manifest as easily as she does.

"Hey Cuz! I just wanted to call and see how you are. I will be home in about a week."

I start to laugh as I hear her speaking with what sounds like a Gaelic accent.

"What are you laughing about?"

"Sorry. It is so funny to hear you talking with a Scottish accent."

"I don't have an accent."

She must have heard herself say that with the accent, because she started laughing, too. I told her about my experiences with Johanna over the last few months.

"So what do you want?" She asks. I can almost see the sparkle in her eyes as she asks.

"Speak it plainly, girl, speak it plainly. Words are creation in action; words attract and words have power. Speak your heart. Choose your words wisely. There is no past and no future. There is only now — this moment. Create this moment as perfectly as you can,"

"Well, I guess I would want joy, love, compassion, and money." I answer skeptically.

"You 'guess' you want joy, love, compassion, and money?"

"OK. I **want** joy, compassion, love, and money."

"How can you speak it with more responsibility and commitment?'

"I don't know what the problem is right now, since I just had an incredible conversation with my guide."

"There are no problems, only opportunities to grow and learn. You pave your reality with your words. In addition, your words mold your experiences. So, use your words to create the now you intend."

I take a deep breath and slowly say, "I am joy, I am love, I am compassion, and I am attracting prosperity in every moment."

"Did you just say the words or did you feel them, too?"

"Okay, give me a minute." I close my eyes and get very clear and calm. I generate a feeling of love and as I feel my heart expanding, I say the words again.

"Much better!" Karen laughs.

"I can't wait to see you, honey! I'll pick you

up at the airport."

"Great! I'll email you my itinerary. Until then, sweetie, work on feeling your wants and numbing the feeling of the things you don't want."

"I will, I promise."

We say our goodbyes and I hang up with a renewed sense of possibility.

Chapter 9

"If you have abandoned one faith, do not abandon all faith. There is always an alternative to the faith we lose. Or is it the same faith under another mask?" Graham Greene

I'm in Coeur d'Alene to shop for groceries and decide to treat myself to a nice lunch. I get out of the car and walk toward a small café, breathing in the cool, crisp air. The first snow of the year usually falls around Thanksgiving and it feels like it's on its way. I love snow and look forward to winter. I step into the restaurant and see a woman at one of the tables who looks very familiar. I step up to the counter and order a sandwich and freshly squeezed juice. I turn around to find a place to sit and I notice the woman again. She looks up to meet my stare and I remember her.

"Hello Jeannie," I say as I approach her table. I can tell she is trying to place who I am. I smile at her and tell her I was at the park to see Johanna.

"Oh," Jeannie responds excitedly, "please join me."

I sit down across from her and she smiles broadly. "So, what did you think of Johanna?"

"I love her. In fact I have spoken with her since the gathering at the park."

"So have I. She's been continuing to work with me on my issues surrounding my father. But I had some of the biggest realizations when I've been alone."

"Would you share your experiences with me?"

"I would love to. Actually, I share my story with everyone who gets within earshot of me. Unfortunately, there are so many people who can't understand what I'm talking about. It's like I'm speaking a different language."

"I know what you mean. It's as though talking about taking responsibility for our creations triggers all of the worst fears in people."

"Exactly!" Jeannie says with a smile. Her eyes are sparkling with joy and understanding. "Oh! I remember you now. You're the one who walked off with Johanna after the riot broke out."

"It turned into a riot?"

"Well, it seemed like a riot. Everyone was mad at everyone else and no one was listening."

I nod, understanding what she meant. "So what have you learned that has changed you so drastically? You no longer look like a scared bunny."

Jeannie laughs and nods her head. "Yeah, you had me pegged perfectly — I *was* like a scared rabbit. Now, everything is so different. I have a sense of peace I've never felt before. Johanna showed me how to look at my father from a whole new perspective.

"Now, instead of blaming him, I feel empathy for him. I know my dad did the best he could. I have finally been able to forgive him. Most importantly, I've forgiven myself. I now know that I create my own experiences — that I'm in charge of my own reality.

"At first, it was hard to stay in the forgiveness. Anger would creep up and I would go into blame, or I would start feeling like I can't do anything right and then beat myself up mentally. The more I worked with Johanna's teachings the more I started taking responsibility for my own life experiences."

"That's wonderful, Jeannie. I admire your ability to just let go."

"Actually, I haven't just let go. I seem to have an ebb and flow with my self-healing. Sometimes I'm strong, certain, and unswerving. Other times I find myself having a pity party and wondering how I could ever be so dense."

"I know exactly what you mean. I find myself doing the same thing. It's almost as though there are two of me and they are both fighting for dominance. Most of the time I can walk myself through the feelings of unworthiness, but sometimes I feel like I'm drowning in my own fears."

Jeannie's eyes have turned within and she nods thoughtfully. After a couple of minutes she looks at me and asks me how I'm doing.

"I find that I'm still struggling with old belief systems I created years ago. My conscious mind wants to let go and live in peace and truth, but my subconscious still wants to replay those old useless recordings that keep me trapped in my present life. I guess I still don't know how to stop following my subconscious mind."

Jeannie shakes her head. "I don't think it's a matter of following your subconscious mind. Johanna told me that everyone thinks they need to reprogram their minds so they can respond 'appropriately' to outside stimuli. The truth is much simpler than that. She explained that the reason people get tangled up in fear and stress is because they aren't being in the present moment."

"So, being in the moment prevents stress and fear?" I am lost in thought as I consider the possibilities. Hmmm, why would that be true? Suddenly, I understand what Johanna meant. "Oh, I get it, Jeannie! If you're not in the present moment, then you must be worrying about the past or the future. I can't count the times I've gone back and thought about an event that happened to me in the past, which then causes me to experience the emotion all over again."

"Right!" Jeannie agrees enthusiastically. "Or you can worry about an event that is going to happen in the future and get so caught up in the feelings that you miss what's going on right now. Plus, I would think that if you are giving energy to a future fear, then all that emotion is actually magnetizing that experience to you."

"Yes," I confirm, "it makes perfect sense. Being in the past or the future will cause you to experience the emotions of that image, which will then override the current experience."

We smile at one another with understanding and then I can't hold in my exuberance any longer. I'm grinning ear to ear as I say, "I *love* this! I love discovering truth and then finding out how it relates to me."

"I know," Jeannie nods with a grin. "I love it, too."

We eat lunch and continue to talk for another hour. As we get up to leave, we give each other a long hug. I feel as though I've known Jeannie all of my life. We swap phone numbers and go on our way.

I am so filled with love and peace that I feel almost buoyant. I walk down the street and I feel like I'm glowing and beautiful. As I pass people on the street they turn to look at me, smiling. I smile back and feel more and more love for everyone and everything. This must be what it's like to experience enlightenment, I think to myself. This must be true loving, true self-awareness. How can I learn to keep this feeling all the time? Is it as simple as staying in the present?

I'm getting into my car when I hear a familiar voice call my name. I turn around to find David approaching. I get the strangest combination of feelings—fear, anger, love, excitement, and dread. I am surprised by the strong emotional reaction, since I haven't thought about David much since I left his house three months ago.

"Hello David," I say as I step back out of my car.

"How are you?" David asks nonchalantly.

"I'm wonderful," I reply as I struggle to keep the love and buoyancy I was experiencing just moments before. "How are you?"

"Good. I'm doing well." He smiles and I can see that he's feeling as nervous as I. "How's Jenny?"

"She's fine. In fact, I'm on my way home so I can be there when she gets home from school."

"Oh, then I won't keep you," he says with a disappointed look.

"That's okay. I have a few minutes to spare. How are Sean and Lisa?"

"They're both doing great. Lisa is graduating next summer and she's trying to decide which school she wants to attend for her masters program."

"Does she still want to be a math teacher?"

"Yes, but she's decided she'd rather not teach secondary math. Lisa wants to teach college students, so now she'll need to get a Ph.D."

"That's great, David. I'm pleased for her."

David nods, looking at me with a sad, faraway expression. I'm feeling more and more uneasy, so I tell David that I need to go. He steps forward to give me a hug and I feel like I'm suffocating. I hug him briefly and then get into the car. I shut the door and roll down the window, feeling much safer.

"Well, take care of yourself," David says softly. "Say hello to Jennifer for me."

"I will," I reply. "Take care, David. Bye."

He watches as I roll up my window and drive off. God! My heart is going to explode! I don't know what to do with all these feelings. The number of different emotions and their intensity overwhelms me.

"How can this be," I say out loud. Just moments before I saw David I was connected to the deepest love I had ever known. Now, I'm sad, angry, and confused. My energy feels completely drained. How can I go from intense joy to intense pain so easily?

Maybe this all has to do with my conversation with Jeannie. If I'm experiencing negative emotions, then I must be dwelling in the past. I'm reliving the past with David; therefore, to feel the love and joy again I need to be in the present moment.

Okay, Deb, so what is true right now? Let's see, I'm driving in the car; it's threatening snow; traffic is light; and I'm playing the radio. I take a deep breath, hoping it will help me relax.

There. I'm feeling better now. I start to sing along with the radio, feeling a little more at ease. All through the twenty-minute drive home I keep catching myself thinking about David and the past. Each time I have to remind myself to stay in the moment.

I get home, bring in the groceries, and start putting them away. Jenny breezes in, drops her backpack and coat on the floor, and yells, "I'm home," as she does every day.

"Hi, honey," I respond. "I'm in the kitchen."

Jenny comes in and gets a snack, telling me all about her day. We chat as I put away the groceries and she finishes her snack. Jenny gets up to leave so she can go out to play, and I notice she's left a mess from her snack.

"Jennifer, don't you **dare** leave your mess for me to clean up!" I'm practically yelling and I startle both of us. The anger that rises is too strong for me to avoid. "I don't need more work to do! I'm busy enough as it is. **Do you understand**?"

"God mom, why are you yelling at me?"

That snaps me back to reality. "I don't know, Jen," I say as calmly as I can, "I'm sorry."

"It's okay, mom," Jenny replies as she comes over and gives me a hug. I hug her back, wondering what had just happened.

Over the next few days, my temper flares with unusual intensity and I can't figure out what's going on. It's that feeling of there being two of me again, and one is fighting with the other to gain control. I don't know what to do and I'm afraid I won't be able to overcome these feelings of anger. The more I try to control my anger and stay in the present moment, the more frustrated I become and the more separated I feel from the love I experienced after my conversation with Jeannie.

It's nearing December and normally I am beginning to get excited about Christmas. There has been a light snow, which usually makes me feel like a kid. This year I just feel dead inside. All of the feelings of love and light are gone and I'm not able to control my emotions. I get up early one snowy morning and get into the tub. Jennifer is at her dad's for the weekend, so I have the house to myself. I close my eyes and pray for help, calling on God, Johanna, Sananda, and any other angels and guides that might be nearby.

"Please help me," I sob aloud. "I don't understand why I can't stay in the love. I have done everything in my power to stay out of the past and future. It seems like the more I concentrate on the present moment, the more out of balance I feel. Please, please help me."

I am weeping uncontrollably from deep within—tears that engulf my entire body and mind and seem to be taking over. I try to stop crying, but there is no respite from the intense emotion that has claimed me. After nearly a half an hour, I manage to get myself out of the bath. I feel drained and sullen. There were no answers to my pleas for help. I am alone—isolated.

The telephone rings and I jump at the sound. "Hello?"

"Hi there."

"Hi Esther. How are you?"

"I'm *wonderful*. How are you?"

"Okay, I guess."

"What's going on? You don't sound good."

"I'm not. I'm having a crisis and I can't seem to get any help from anyone or anywhere. I feel isolated, alone, and unloved."

"Wow. It sounds like you're really hurting."

"Yes, I am," I sniffle, trying not to start crying again.

"Tell me about it."

I proceed to tell Esther about the emotions of the last couple weeks. "I just can't figure out what triggered it."

"Well, when was the last time you felt good?"

I tell her about my experience with Jeannie and about all of the insights we had gained and about how much love I felt for all of life.

"Did anything else happen between that day and now that might have changed your energy so drastically?"

"I can't think of anything. Oh, I saw David right after I left the restaurant from having lunch with Jeannie."

"Really? Tell me what happened."

I proceeded to tell Esther about my run-in with David, and how I've been working on forgiving him and myself for the breaking up of the relationship.

"You know," I start, "it seems like the more I try to forgive, the more bitter I feel."

"Aha! That's what you need to look at. Apparently, you're not ready to forgive either David or yourself. Something else is in the way. You need to discover what that is so you can heal it. My guess is that you're still angry."

"Maybe you're right. I'll look at that."

We talk a little longer and Esther tells me

she's going to be out of town for a few days. When we hang up, I think about the conversation.

Well, if I'm angry then the forgiveness exercise should be working. But it's **not** working. I just keep getting more depressed. I nearly holler my prayer: 'God, *please* help me. I don't know what else to do. Johanna, I need you.' I start to cry again in frustration.

The phone rings again and I struggle to contain my tears so I can answer.

"H-hello?"

Steve's voice is on the other end. "Deborah? Are you okay?"

"No, I'm not okay. I can't get back to the loving state I was experiencing. The harder I try to return to the love, the farther I get away from it. It seems to have all started after running into David a couple of weeks ago. I've been trying to forgive him and myself, but it just makes me feel worse.

"I had a conversation with a friend about staying in the present moment and not letting the past or future take over the present. I figured that all of my intense emotion was about the past and I needed to stay in the 'here and now' to let go of the feelings. But it's not working. I feel worse every day. I've been praying for help, but I'm being ignored. I don't know what else to do."

"It sounds to me like you need to do some anger work. You can't forgive before you release the anger. That's a little like putting the cart before the horse. Remember, the body stores trauma. I suggest that you get out into nature and let the anger come up. Feel it and release it. Then you will be able to surrender to peace."

"I've always believed that when an emotion, like anger, comes up you're not supposed to engage in it. What you're saying seems contradictory to that belief."

"No, it's not. Look at it this way: you're in the mall and some kids run into you, knocking you to the ground. You get up, feeling angry. Now you have a choice. You can be angry with those kids and yell at them, or you can smile and not get angry.

"Now, think about this: You are in a relationship and you feel mentally and physically abused. You do everything in your power to keep from accepting the invitation to get angry, but it doesn't help you. You are feeling wounded inside and out. Now you have a choice. You can release the anger and free your body of the trauma so you can forgive, or you can stuff the pain and gloss it over and keep the anger buried alive."

"So you are saying that in order to stay in the present moment, I need to recognize and heal any old stored pain because it can hinder my journey to forgiveness."

"Yes, but remember: even though there is pain that happened in the past, you don't want to get caught up there. It happened. It's over. It's not true anymore. The only thing that is true is that you have created a story around that situation. The past isn't even relevant anymore. The only thing that affects you now is the story about it. Figure out what you decided was true about it."

"Thanks, Steve. I'll go right now and see what I can bring up. I'll call you later and let you know how it goes. I love you."

"Love you, too. Bye."

Chapter 10

"He who knows others is clever; He who knows himself has discernment." Lao-Tzu

Living near a lake has its advantages. A friend loaned me his kayak, and I love to go out on the lake this time of year. The lake hasn't iced over yet, and all of the summer people have gone. It's a quiet, restful time that I love. I load the kayak into the back of my car and drive down to the lake. The lake is deserted, so I know I'll have it all to myself. I navigate to the far side of the lake where there are no homes and I drag the kayak out of the water. I hike across the snowy ground to a secluded spot in the trees where the snow could not penetrate.

I find a dead tree, pick up an old limb, and proceed to pace back and forth in front of the tree. I start to talk to the tree as though it's David. The more I talk, the angrier I feel. Soon, I'm yelling and crying my pain and frustration. I take the limb I've been holding and I start hitting the dead tree. The more I strike it, the more my anger grows in intensity.

Finally exhausted, I let go of the limb and drop to my knees. I begin to sob and I hurt so badly inside that I feel like I'm dying. I spend a half an hour crying off and on and it's almost as though I'm retching each time the tears come.

Finally, drained and exhausted, I get into the kayak and paddle to the middle of the lake. I close my eyes and allow myself to drift on the calm, cold water. I feel drained, but I also feel lighter and freer.

As I make my way back to shore, I see a lone figure standing on the beach. The bright sun makes the woman look as though she's glowing. As I approach the shore I can see it is Johanna. She is smiling brightly, yet I feel angry with her.

"Hello!" Johanna calls as she waves to me.

"Hi Johanna," I answer quietly as the kayak slides onto the sand. I step out of the kayak and pull it up under a tree where the grass is protected from the snow. Johanna sits down on the grass and motions for me to join her. I pull the skirt off the kayak and sit on it to stay dry. I am feeling uncomfortable.

"Tell me what's on your mind," Johanna says with a gentle smile.

When I look at Johanna, I find it impossible to stay angry with her. "I have been praying and asking for help for days," I start, looking down. "It felt like you and Sananda had abandoned me. No one responded to my plea, no one offered any help whatsoever. I was completely alone and in pain."

"Dearest Deborah, you were never alone. We are always with you, even when you can't see or feel us. You cannot be separated from us or from Love. Remember, we are all of the same light, the same love, and the same energy.

"Imagine life as a big, beautiful tapestry. Every being, whether alive or in spirit is a thread within that tapestry. You can pull out a thread, but it leaves a bare spot in the tapestry's design. It takes every being to make up this tapestry.

"You seem to understand and appreciate the nature of life on many levels and yet you deny it on others. I can come to you and give you all the answers to your problems every time you call, but how would that serve you?"

"What do you mean?"

"If I supply you with the answers to the problems you face, will you learn how to solve problems?"

"No, I guess not. But I wasn't asking you to solve my problems, I was asking for help in solving them for myself. But there was no answer from any of you."

"You don't think your prayer was answered? Didn't Esther call soon after your prayer and offer you insights into your pain? And when you still could not grasp the insights that Esther offered, didn't Steve call you as soon as you asked for further assistance?

"Were you asking for truth or were you asking for someone to help you feel better? You were being offered words of truth by two of your closest friends, but you couldn't respond appropriately because you hadn't released the emotion behind the pain you were experiencing. No one — human nor spirit will rescue you from yourself. You must find your own way, which will empower you."

I shake my head. "I'm confused. Why couldn't the intense love I felt after my conversation with Jeannie be sustained even though I saw David? Why wasn't that feeling of love able to conquer the pain? Why was I abandoned? I thought that Love would always intervene and assist us when we pray."

"*You* are the essence of Love in every single moment. You are free to choose the outcome of any situation. To put it another way, you are free to select the outcome of any scene in your life drama.

"However, your body is human and it stores human emotion like a battery holds a charge. You can make the conscious choice not to react from emotion, but once you have acquired an emotion you must release it through right action. Right action means to treat the emotional pain holistically — as part of the mind *and* body. The human muscles store trauma and the human mind records and reenacts painful memories."

"So, you're saying that I had stored emotion and pain regarding David, and when I saw him again I began to replay the memories?"

"Yes. This is where the forgiveness work comes in. You must learn to forgive all the players in your trauma drama. Forgive David, forgive yourself, and forgive all the times you've hurt inside because you were certain that you had been forsaken."

I nod in understanding. "And Love can't forsake me because I'm the essence of Love."

"Correct."

"And when I learn how to stop accepting emotional trauma as a way of life, then I can live as the essence of Love all the time.

"Yes. Remember, if you are in pain you are being given an opportunity to learn a truth about yourself. Don't run or hide from pain with denial or drugs or liquor. Offer loving kindness, gentleness, and acceptance to yourself as well as to the rest of life. Be at peace with yourself. Trust yourself to make the right decisions. Johanna starts to fade again as she says, "Go in peace, dear one."

I watch her disappear as I sit motionless on the shore of the lake. A gentle snow starts to fall, and I can feel the tiny flakes land on my face and then melt away. I sit there for a long time, trying to piece together all of the information I have received.

I load up the kayak, and then head back home, determined to learn these lessons and to understand how I create my experiences. The idea that I store pain makes so much sense to me. It also helps me understand why sometimes my emotions seem to be on autopilot.

Chapter 11

"When you have to make a choice and don't make it, that in itself is a choice." William James

I drive up to the house and start to unload the kayak when Diane's car pulls up. "Hey you! How are you?"

I'm good, Diane, how are you?"

"I'm great! Listen, there's no volleyball tonight, so a bunch of us are going to the Winter Carnival. Want to join us?"

"I'd love to. Jenny's with her dad, so I'll have no curfew!"

"Let's go together. I'll pick you up at 4:00, ok?"

"Sounds great. I'll see you then."

Diane and I get to the gate and most of the gang is already there. We all head inside and proceed to have the time of our lives. We play games and look at the exhibits.

Around 7:00 a band starts to play in a huge barn and we all head over to see what it's about. A blues band is playing and there's dancing. At least 10 of us decide to stay and dance. Before I can sit down at the benches we found, one of my friends asks me to dance. I dance with several of the guys and then plop into my chair all sweaty and exhilarated.

I glance around at the group, smiling. Kathy shoots me an odd look and as I stare at her, trying to figure out her expression, I see what her look is all about. While I was on the dance floor, David had joined us.

My heart skips a beat and I feel lightheaded. Diane leans over and apologizes, saying he wasn't invited to join us—he just found us. I pat her hand and tell her it's all right.

"I've been doing a lot of work to release the pain I feel toward him. So I guess this will be a good experiment."

Diane looks at me doubtfully, and then nods and gives me a hug. Jim asks her to dance and I watch them head to the dance floor. I close my eyes so I can check my barometer—how *do* I feel about this? I don't feel angry anymore and I don't feel sad… I feel sort of excited and shaky.

Kathy comes and sits by me, putting her arm around my shoulder. I hug her back and she asks me if I'm okay.

"Yeah, I think so," I say. But my mouth feels full of cotton balls. "I just don't know what I'll do if he asks me to dance."

"You don't have to dance with him, Deb. Just say no if he asks."

"Actually, I'm curious about it. I've been doing a lot of forgiveness work and I wonder how I feel toward him now."

"Just be careful, sweetie," she says, as she gets up to dance with her boyfriend, Bill.

I nod and watch them walk to the dance floor.

⬅

My mind wanders and I remember how good it felt when David and I danced. He dances really well and when we slow danced it was like our bodies were made for each other. I can remember how much he enjoyed it when I sang along to the music as we danced in each other's arms.

➡

I am brought back to the present by someone speaking to me. As I look up I see David. He's asking me to dance. My jaw drops and I just stare at him for a moment. He starts to straighten like he's going to walk away and I stand up. He looks surprised, but it's obvious he's also very pleased with my decision. It's a fast dance, I reason to myself; it should be safe enough. I feel so nervous as I follow him to the dance floor — I can hardly breathe.

While we dance to the song I close my eyes

and get lost in the music. When the song ends, they immediately go right into a slow number. I start to turn to walk away and David holds out his hand.

"I-I don't know, David, if I want to dance anymore," I stammer as my cheeks redden.

"Just one more, Deb."

I look at him and feel very uncomfortable. What am I doing here? I need to go sit down *right now*. But then that little voice inside of me whispers, 'yes, but don't you want to see how it feels to be near him again?'

I swallow hard, and trembling, I take his hand. As we dance cheek to cheek, all of the feelings I had for him well up inside of me. I am shocked at how good it feels to be in his arms again and how much I still care for him.

Great. Now I know why I stayed angry. As long as I was angry I didn't have to face the fact that I still love him. What do I do with this information now? It's obvious we weren't meant to be together. I think of the old saying, 'can't live with him, and can't live without him.'

After the dance I walk away, out of the dance area and out into the night. I have to get my thoughts together. David follows me out and asks to talk with me. My stomach is full of butterflies and I'm afraid to look him in the eyes.

"Deb, I've done a lot of thinking and I want

you to know how wrong I was. I made a commitment and I reneged. I apologize."

I stop dead in my tracks and look at him. His face is sincere and I believe him. "I guess I am to blame, too. I stormed off instead of talking it through with you."

"No, Deb, I wouldn't have listened… I couldn't have listened then. I was so afraid."

"Afraid of what?"

"Afraid of you, of us, of the commitment, of the possibility of happiness, of the possibility of failure… of everything."

"So what are you saying?"

"I don't know exactly. I just want you to know how wrong I was and how I wish things could be different between us. I know it's not possible, but I…I wish we could start over."

"Oh, David, I-I can't even think about that now."

David rushes to answer. "I know. I'm not asking you to. I'm just telling you what my heart feels—not my head and my logic."

"Thanks, but I can't do anything with that information right now. I just need some time. I need time to think."

"I respect that. I'll leave you alone now." David turns to walk away, and then glances back. "Thanks for hearing me out. See you at volleyball next week."

I nod and he leaves. I walk through the fairgrounds not seeing anything. I'm trying so hard to understand my emotional and physical response to him. Apparently, I still love him, but it's obvious he's not good for me. There were so many problems when we lived together. Could we have worked them out? Part of me thinks we could have, and part of me senses there is more to the picture than I know.

The cold finally penetrates and I realize I walked out without my jacket. As I head back, I begin to worry that David is still there. I just can't take any more tonight. I really wanted a night free of my drama.

When I return to the tables, David is gone. I think about staying, but my heart just isn't into it anymore.

Chapter 12

"Half the work that is done in this world is to make things appear what they are not." Elias Root Beadle

The last few months have been interesting. I have seen David at volleyball and we have been spending more and more time talking like we used to. I can see how hard he's trying to break old patterns and I can see he loves me deeply.

I too have done a lot of work to understand myself and the things that trigger me. I can see that I also love David deeply. This feels very scary because of our past, but it also feels right since we are looking so honestly at ourselves.

One of the conversations that we have fairly regularly is the issue of trust. David has a lot of fear when it comes to trusting others. He wants to trust more than anything, but something always seems to undermine his ability to do so. When an issue comes up between us and it's obvious it's trust-related, we sit and talk it through until he feels more comfortable with me again.

On a crisp and clear April morning, David and I are on a hike through an ancient cedar grove that I love. I stop at one of the oldest trees in the grove and give it a hug. I love to hug trees…I can really feel their energy and wisdom.

David waits patiently (he's not a tree hugger), and then as I step away, he asks me to sit down so we can talk. We find a log and sit down.

David fidgets nervously, and then he looks me in the eyes and asks me to marry him.

My heart seems to stop; and then it races so fast I can hardly catch my breath. "What?"

"I know it's a big step, Deb, and I know how unsure you must feel right now. Just think about it before you answer, okay?"

My insides are churning and arguing. One part is telling me to run like the wind from this man. The other is telling me to face my fears and to recognize and respond to the love I feel for him. I sit there and stare at him, totally paralyzed by the internal conflict. Suddenly, something inside of me screams, 'take a chance!' I lunge into his arms and say yes.

"But I have one stipulation," I say, as I lean back and look into his eyes. "I want that one-year commitment first."

"But wouldn't it be a commitment in itself to marry?"

"Maybe. But the rest of our life together is too important to rush into anything. One year. Then I'll marry you. In the meantime, I will live with you."

We continued the conversation over the next few days, and I finally agree to move in with him and then to marry him in January instead of the following summer.

I move into David's home in the country once again, and to the credit of all our friends, everyone wishes us well in spite of our recent history. David and I make an agreement to treat the relationship as though we are already married, and one of those steps includes opening a joint checking account. We open a CD account for the wedding with extra income we have made throughout the year.

My freelance writing work, which had been prolific for six months, suddenly dries up and there is no work. I search every day for work and eventually, have to start looking for work in town. Driving back and forth to Spokane in the winter isn't an exciting prospect, but I have to do something. Fortunately, just as I am about to accept a position in town, I get an offer to write my own book. My own book! I am so thrilled (and relieved) that I will be able to stay at home and work.

There are two reasons why I like working at home: I enjoy not having to fight traffic and weather, and most importantly, I like being available for my daughter or her school. Now I can be there for Sean, too.

I receive my first advance right away, and I go to work. I finish half of the book in just six weeks and receive my second advance. Everyone is happy with my work and with my ability to beat my deadlines.

In the meantime, David, Sean, Jennifer, and I settle into a family routine. It takes some time to adjust parenting styles, since Sean has different expectations from his father than Jennifer has from me. Also, Jennifer and I don't eat meat so I end up having to cook two similar dinners every night — one with meat and one without. I don't mind the cooking since I love to cook, but handling the meat is a challenge.

David has strange little flare-ups in temper from time to time, but nothing serious and we are always able to talk through the problem. We grow closer and closer and I begin to realize a love deeper than any I have ever known before. When I look into his eyes and he gazes back at me with total glowing love, I feel so much love that it actually hurts. It's like I am about to explode.

The months pass and Lisa is soon home for Christmas break. We have a lot in common and enjoy great talks. Christmas is fantastic. We all share and laugh and eat and talk; and I look around from time to time to absorb what a wonderful family we make.

One day I'm sitting at the table with Sean, helping him with an advanced Trigonometry problem. When we are all done and he leaves to go watch TV, I remember my dream of several months earlier. Maybe it was a precognitive dream. Maybe some part of me realized we would all be together again.

The closer the wedding day came; the more flare-ups David seems to be having. I get the feeling he is holding something back, but he insists it is only pre-wedding jitters.

The wedding is planned for January 11, so we can go on our honeymoon in Acapulco during my birthday. The day before the wedding, all of our family and friends fly in and we reserve a block of rooms in the same resort where the wedding is planned. We all meet for dinner together and have a wonderful time. My heart is so filled with love for these people and for the step I am about to take that I know what perfection feels like.

The wedding is scheduled for 4:00 p.m. with a formal dinner and reception afterward. The morning of the wedding, David comes to my room and wants to talk. He admits there is something bothering him and he needs to talk it out with me before we go any further.

He says that he has two things to discuss with me. He asks that I hear both concerns out before I respond, and I agree.

"Look, Deb, I have so much invested in my home and property that I need to feel that my livelihood and investment are protected. I want you to sign a prenuptial agreement that states that if the marriage doesn't work out, I keep my home and property."

It's all I can do not to scream. There it is again: the TRUST demon. Instead, I take a deep breath and hold my tongue so he can finish as we agreed.

"Secondly," he continues, "I have really tried to come to terms with this, but I just can't agree to have your parents live on the property with us."

That's it! No more tongue holding. "You know how I feel about having my parents close to me. And now, on our wedding day you tell me you don't even trust me or believe our marriage will last? How can you do this to me? How dare you!"

"I know it's a shock and it's sudden, but this is important to me. I have the papers right here."

I am the most peaceful, nonviolent person you'll ever know, but in that moment I see red. I stand up, grab the prenuptial agreement, and rip it up. David stands up, too, his eyes wide. I go over to him and slug his arm with my fists and scream, "How can you do this to me now? How can you hit me with this today?"

He grabs my wrists and looks at me, but before he can say a word, I wrench free and run out of the room and down to the lake. It is cold and the snow is seeping into my sneakers, but I don't even feel it. I am so hurt and angry. I begin to cry convulsively.

What am I going to do? He is changing all the rules, but he waits until it is too late for me to react. Everyone is here for a wedding. He knew that if he waited, I would be more likely to agree to his terms. After a few minutes, he walks up and wants to talk about it.

"Do you still want these changes?" I ask.

He nods, and starts to speak, but before he can, I whirl around and face him, my face burning from the tears on my cold face. "Then the wedding is off!"

I run away, sobbing, get in my car and drive away to think so he can't follow me. I pull into a nearby park and stop the car. Everything feels upside down. What do I do now? Pull out? Everyone is here and between us we have already spent $3,000 of the money we put away for the wedding. Nothing makes sense about David anymore. I go back to the resort and tell my parents.

They tell me not to worry about them—they are perfectly fine where they are in California. But as far as the prenuptial agreement, they can't advise me. Mom sits on the bed and holds me as I cry. It isn't fine with me. None of it is fine with me.

There is a knock on the door and when Dad opens it, David is standing there. "Hello,

George. I need to talk to Deborah."

Dad opens the door wider and says, "Come on, Esther, let's go have breakfast and let them talk."

Mom looks at me, still in her arms, and I look back, not certain I want to see him. She kisses me on the forehead, gives me a 'whatever you decide is all right' look, stands up and walks out with Dad.

David steps in and shuts the door. I sit there, rigid and angry. David stands by the door as though he doesn't know what to do. He finally walks over and sits down in the chair across from the bed.

"I apologize for hitting you with this today. I should have talked it over with you a long time ago."

I look at him sullenly, feeling very beat up inside. "I guess so."

"So let's talk about it now. I have thought about it and maybe we can come to some agreements. Would it be possible to have your parents live a little farther away, like on the hill where the horse corral used to be? They would still be close, but we would have some privacy and I wouldn't have to look at their prefab house out my windows. I have to be honest here, Deb, I moved onto so much acreage for the privacy."

"Why didn't you say that before? Why did

you have to make it sound like a unilateral decision that they couldn't even be there?"

"I don't know. I think I started to feel panicked and hemmed in. The closer it got to the wedding, the more panicked I felt and then for some reason, the more I was afraid to tell you. I know what it means to have your parents with you."

"What about the prenuptial agreement? Where did that come from?"

"I'm scared, Deb. I don't want to lose everything I've worked for all my life."

"And just how do I pose a threat to 'everything you've worked for all your life'? How can you know so little about who I am after a year and a half?"

"I know who you are. I know you'd never hurt a fly. I know you'd give your last morsel of food if you saw a person who was starving. I know all of that. But what I don't know is how you'd react if we split up and you were hurt and angry."

"How did I react when we split up last year? Did I try to take anything that didn't belong to me?" I asked. David shook his head in response. "What about the things we had accumulated together or I bought for you as a gift? Did I take more than my share?"

"No. You took less than I expected."

"So? What's the problem here?"

"We weren't married then. You didn't have the legal right to half of everything I owned."

I sigh, feeling very frustrated. "So, I want to marry you for your home and money."

"No, I know that's not it."

"Then what is it?" I ask exasperatedly.

"I *don't know*." He answers emphatically.

"Why are you condemning our marriage to failure before it has even begun? Why do you worry we won't stay married on our wedding day? Why don't you trust me—us—our love—enough to work things out?"

"I want to, Deb, I really want to. But my last two marriages failed, so I'm afraid that this one will, too."

"You can't compare one relationship to another. You can't compare your ex-wives to me. One thing has nothing to do with the other. They are very different people. It would have been different."

"Would have been? So you're still calling off the wedding?"

"No, David, you are—through your fear and irrational need to protect yourself from me and my family." I stood up and walked to the door. With my hand and eyes on the knob, I said, "I don't really have anything else to say, except how deeply sad and hurt I feel. This was going to be the most important day of my life and the beginning of a whole new part of my life." Suddenly overcome with the weight of what was happening, I bury my face in my hands and start to sob.

"Oh, Deborah," David says as he stands and walks up to me. "I am so sorry." He starts to put his arms around me to console me, but I shrug him off. He drops his arms, but continues to stand there.

"Please help me. I don't want to ruin our love." He begins to cry and is so embarrassed that he turns away.

We both stand there lost in our own grief when I realize what he had said. I look over and see him for the first time. He is crying. I can see the scared little boy and the grown man all at once, and my heart goes out to him. I walk over to him and we grab each other for dear life. He rescinds the prenup and we agree to continue with the ceremony.

I am in the bride's ready room with my bride's maids as we dress and talk. There is a knock at the door and Diane answers it, since the only thing I have on so far is my merry widow. It's my brother, Dana. He insists on speaking with me, so I wrap a towel around me and we step into the bathroom.

Dana is handsome and charismatic and the ladies love him. He looks stunning in his suit with his graying temples and jet black hair.

"Look, mom and dad told me what happened. You don't have to feel obligated to continue with the wedding just because everyone is here. We can turn it into a great party instead."

I feel so much love for him in that moment, that I give him a hug. "It's ok, sweetie, we have worked it out and I am ready to marry him."

"Are you sure?

I nod and smile, and he gives me a hug and leaves.

As I walk down the aisle in my wedding gown, I am terrified. Part of me feels like I am doing the right and perfect thing because I love him so deeply. The other part remembers the events of the past hours and wonder if this marriage will grow and thrive. I have a dull headache from all the stress.

The reception is a wonderful party of food, friends, family, and dancing. However, my headache won't go away no matter how much aspirin I take. I have never had a headache like this before.

The next morning we have breakfast with our families before leaving on our honeymoon. My dad and David's dad are head to head talking about science and engineering. It's so cool that they like each other.

They see us off and we head to the airport. The flight was uneventful, except for the headache that hasn't gone away.

There are subtle and not so subtle changes in David during our honeymoon. It's like there is another person emerging that I never knew existed. Sometimes the honeymoon is like heaven on earth and at other times it is as though I am with a stranger. And I'm still suffering off and on from the headache.

One day, he picks at me unmercifully. That evening he doesn't like what I am planning to wear. We are going to a street fair and I want to be comfortable, so I have on a pair of stretchy shorts and a tee shirt. I fix my hair neatly, and when I come out he complains about my outfit.

"You don't normally dress like that."

"I know, David, but I'm a little uncomfortable," I said, as I pat my tummy. "It must be all the traveling, stress, and new foreign food."

"But I don't want you to dress like that. I want to be proud of you and show you off. Everyone else will be dressed nicer."

We go around and around. Finally, despite my discomfort, I change. I'm angry that he can't allow me to dress the way I want to. I'm angry with myself for giving in...but I know that if I hadn't, the argument would have never stopped.

When we get to the street fair I start pointing out all of the women who are dressed as I wanted to dress (unfortunately, most of them are overweight and I'm not).

After about six or seven women David retorts, "Yeah, and that's how you would've looked."

I stop dead in my tracks and just stare at him. I can't believe it. This isn't the first time he has insulted me since the wedding. I turn and walk away into a crowd of tourists. I know he is probably trying to catch up to me, but I need to be alone. I walk for at least an hour, trying to sort out all that had been happening. I don't like this new David—he is acting rude.

His behavior intensifies as the days pass and I want to leave him and go home—during our honeymoon!

The new year brings other difficulties as well. When we get home from the honeymoon I finish the book and receive my final advance. All that is left to do are the author reviews, the table of contents, and the glossary. I have already been offered another book and the timing would have worked out perfectly... *would have* worked out perfectly. Unfortunately, the test on which the first book was based had been removed from the market and is being completely rewritten. This means that some of my chapters might not be pertinent to the new test.

I wait for what seems like an eternity (actually only a week) to finally have all of my fears realized: the test has major changes and almost half of my book will have to be rewritten. To make matters worse, the way the contract I signed with the publishers is worded, I will receive no additional money for the rewrites!

Needless to say, I can't accept the new book offer and David's and my finances will be severely effected. David's salary will temporarily have to cover both of our debts and I have large student loan payments on top of my normal debt. This causes a strain that I could never have predicted.

When I work at home, I get up and get ready as though I have a job outside of the house. I start to work at 8:00 when the house is quiet and everyone has left for the day. I stop for lunch for one hour and then I go back to work until 4:00, when I stop to visit with the kids, watch our favorite show together, and start dinner.

I have been working feverishly to finish the book, but there are new obstacles cropping up every week. I start to rewrite a chapter and then I am informed by the publishers that the test crashed in that area, so technicians are rewriting the question! Or, I'll get a chapter done and send it off with all the text and screen shots, only to be told the screen shots don't work because they've decided to change the image format. Frustration is mounting, I am working longer and longer hours to get done, and on top of it, David is changing, too. I know the finances are concerning him and I am feeling very guilty for not being able to contribute.

I try to help in other ways, like keeping the wood box filled. On my lunch break, I'll often go out and split wood and make kindling and I'll shovel the snow from the walk and porch. Just before David gets home I'll light candles and make the kids clean up their messes in the living room.

In spite of my long hours I continue to make dinner and keep the house clean, but my efforts never seem to be good enough. He often cleans a room, like the kitchen or bathroom after I finish with it.

After the kids help with the dinner dishes and they go off to play, I go over the counters and table again to make sure everything is clean. Tonight, after I make dinner and do the dishes, I walk into the kitchen and he is cleaning the floor with a vegetable brush.

"I already cleaned the kitchen, David."

He sweeps his arms about the room and says, "You call this clean?"

I look around the kitchen. The floor is swept and spot cleaned, the pots are washed and put away, the dishwasher is humming, the counters and sink are clean, and the leftovers are in the fridge. The kids even cleaned the refrigerator doors because they noticed their fingerprints were all over them.

I give him a puzzled look. "Yes. I call this clean."

"Well I don't. If you cared, you'd make sure everything was clean when I get home. I work hard all day and I don't need this."

"And I don't work hard all day?"

"You're home all day. You're here to make sure everything is done."

"I'm home, but I'm also working. What do you think I do all day, sit around and smoke cigarettes and watch soap operas?" I say sarcastically (and no, I don't smoke *or* watch soap operas).

"Frankly, I'm not sure what you do."

I start to get really angry and I try to control it. I start to explain exactly what I do all day. Suddenly, he throws down the brush and stomps towards me. He starts yelling at me and calling me terrible, terrible names. I see the kids out of the corner of my eye peeking over the banister to see what's going on.

I get so flustered that I just stand there. After he storms away to finish the floor I walk away, slip on my snow boots, and go outside in the night for a walk. He calls me back, saying not to walk away on him. I walk into the snowy woods and end up getting so lost in thought that I'm gone over an hour before I know it. I start out of the woods and onto the road. I can hear Jennifer calling for me... poor thing she must be worried! I left her and Sean in the house after that exhibition David put on.

I walk up on the porch and take off my boots. As I step inside, Jenny grabs and hugs me. I kiss the top of her head and tell her I'm all right. Sean is there, too, looking worried and I caress his cheek and nod that it's okay. He smiles and then he and Jenny go back to getting ready for bed.

David must be upstairs in our room, so I sit down on the couch and continue to try and make sense of his personality changes. He comes downstairs and welcomes me back as though nothing has happened. He sits next to me on the couch and wants a hug. I lean away from him and he looks at me with a puzzled look.

"Are you still mad?" He asks in an innocent tone.

"Of course I feel angry, David. No one has ever spoken to me in that way before."

"It's just how I vent. It's nothing serious."

"Well, I don't agree. It felt very serious and very hurtful. That form of venting is not okay with me. Find another outlet besides me or the kids."

"I would never hurt the kids."

"You just hurt me... and the kids were listening and that hurts them as well."

"God, Deb, don't be so sensitive."

It is clear he has no idea why his words and actions hurt me so much, but we continue the conversation and he promises to try and change the behavior. As the days pass, David's behavior becomes more and more irrational. Some days, no matter how much I try to stay calm and talk him through his feelings, he is bound and determined to get into a fight. He always ends up calling me terrible names or throwing something across the room.

After each fight is over, he comes over and acts like the incident never happened. My headaches have turned into migraines and I can't control them anymore. I am on strong medication to combat them, but end up getting Demerol shots at least once or twice a month to disconnect my brain from my body for a while.

It's mid-April and we are going to Spokane Valley to celebrate Sean's birthday at this cool party place for kids. They have video and pinball games, bumper cars, a batting cage, and many other games.

I head outside after breakfast to take a short walk in the perfumed spring morning, enjoying all the different spring flower smells. David catches up with me and starts to walk beside me. I look at him and I know immediately by his expression that he wants to start a fight.

"I can't believe you are out here when the house needs to be cleaned. I am certainly not doing it all alone."

I looked at him, surprised, and said, "What needs to be done?"

He looks at me with anger in his face and says, "Everything!"

"Ok, there is no need to get upset or raise your voice. I'm happy to help do whatever needs to be done before we leave." I keep my voice calm, hoping to avoid another nasty fight.

"Well, let's go then! Right now!"

"If you insist, but I think it will still be there in 10 minutes. I would like to finish my walk first, and we don't leave for several hours."

His face reddened and he was nearly shaking with anger. "I want to start right now. It might take that long to clean up."

"Ok, David, we'll go back now. Please try to stay calm. Let's not do anything to ruin this day for Sean."

That was all it took. I was trying to soothe him, but that was not what he wanted—he wanted to fight—he *needed* to fight for some reason. He was practically screaming at me now.

"Are you saying that I want to ruin my son's birthday?! Is that what you are saying? That I'm a terrible father who would ruin everything for him?"

I just look at him. Anything I say now will only inflame the situation to an even greater degree. I turn and start walking toward the house, saying, "I'll start in the bedroom."

He storms up to me, grabs my arm and whirls me around to face him. He looks like a wild animal and now I am afraid of him— perhaps that's what he wanted all along. If I am afraid of him, then he is in charge and in control.

"Don't walk away on me," he seethes.

At that moment, he got what he wanted all along...he wanted to bait me until I could no longer keep myself calm and unfortunately, it worked, because now I am angry.

"David, **let go of me**. You are hurting my arm," I say as I try to jerk my arm from his grip. "I just wanted to do what you asked."

He releases me so violently that he hurts my arm. He continues to glare at me like he could kill me right there.

"Are you happy now?" I say loudly. "You wanted to trigger me so we could fight and you were successful. I am now angry. Are we done *now*? Can I go to the house *now*?"

"Fine!" He screams as he wheels around and stomps off.

I look toward the house and the kids are watching from Sean's bedroom window. Even from out here I can see the terror on their faces. Great, now that will be on their minds instead of looking forward to the party.

We clean up the already clean house and I go to the bathroom to get ready. Instead of feeling light and happy, I feel heavy and sullen. As predicted, David walks up to me all smiles and light and wants a hug and kiss. He got his fight and now he's happy. Apparently, I am his release valve.

I push him away, saying that I need to get ready to go. He starts to get upset again, but before he can strike, the kids come in and want to know what time we are leaving. Thankfully, David walks out.

We pile into the car and head down the dirt driveway. Sean and Jenn seem to be happy and excited in the back, talking away about what they want to do at the party. David looks me up and down and shakes his head. I look down and I don't see anything wrong.

"What is it, David?"

"You look like shit."

"Excuse me?" I respond in surprise.

"I think I will leave you out in the middle of nowhere and let you find your way back on your own. With the way you look, I think you'll fit right in with those back woods crazies."

"Let me out of the car, David, I will take Jenn—and Sean, if he wants to come, in my own car and I'll meet you there."

"No," is all he replies.

"Let me out now."

Silence.

"*David...*" is all I get out because he looks at me like he's gone mad.

I shove the car into park and it jerks to a sudden stop. Now he's livid and I am trying to open the car door to get out. "Come on kids," I say as I open the door.

He grabs the front of my shirt and slaps me so hard that he knocks out a lens from my sunglasses. Then he screams, "You could have ruined the transmission, you stupid bitch!"

I wrench free and stumble out of the car. Just as I reach for the back door handle to let the kids out, he floors it and the car spits up dirt and gravel in my face as the car slips and slides down the driveway toward the highway. I can hear the kids screaming and I bolt down the driveway after them, still choking on the dust and rock.

He is in an uncontrolled skid as he slides onto the highway, barely missing a logging truck full of logs. That must have scared him, because he pulls onto the shoulder just as I get there. I rip open the car door and Jennifer flies into my arms, shaking and sobbing. I look at Sean and he is white with fear. As I reach my arm out for him, David whirls around, angry anew, and grabs Sean's arm.

"No! My son stays with me."

Sean turns and looks at him with a withering stare. He jerks his arm free, stares at his father, and with tears in his eyes he says in a near whisper, "Leave me alone, dad." I can see he is still shaking from the fright as he climbs out of the car.

"We are going in my car, David. Show up at the party or don't—I really don't care anymore."

I turn and head back up the driveway with my arms around each of the kids. We hear David spin out on the shoulder as he tries to make a fast getaway.

When we get back up the driveway to the house, I have the kids sit on a big rock for a minute and we talk. I want to make sure they are ok—physically and mentally. They are obviously still very shaken, but Sean wants to try and get to the party since his friends are all there waiting for him. Jenn is willing to go, too, but I get the feeling it is mostly for Sean.

We get in my car and head down the road. We are so late by this time that I decide to take a back road shortcut. It is all dirt and gravel, but it cuts nearly 10 miles off the trip. We had been on the road about 10 minutes when we round a corner and see a big, older Cadillac straddling a gully between the road and forest. As I slow down we can see a little old lady behind the wheel, completely terrified. The gully is about eight or nine feet deep.

I pull over and the kids and I get out. I climb down the gully and up to the other side. I approach her car and I see her front tires are not on solid ground. In addition, they are slammed against the dirt rise, which keeps the tires slightly over the gulley. I climb back to the road again and I try to look in without touching the car. The woman looks exhausted and both of her hands are gripping the wheel so tightly that they are white. As I look around I see the transmission is still in Drive and both feet are pressing on the brake so hard that her legs are shaking. The driver side door is over the gully, so I can't get to her or get her out.

She looks at me through the half-closed window and says in a shaky voice, "I-I can't hold on much longer."

"You are doing great. What is your name?"

"Vi-Violet," she breathes.

Can you slowly take your right hand off of

the steering wheel and put the car in park?"

She shakes her head slowly, with fear in her eyes.

"It's okay, Violet. Your left hand will keep the wheel still. Just loosen the grip of your right hand... Good! See? Your car didn't budge. Now can you put it into park?"

She takes her right hand, grasps the gear shift lever on the steering column and eases it into park. Violet purses her lips and slowly lets out the breath she was holding.

"That's great, Violet. Do you know where your parking brake is located?"

She nods and glances down at the floor near the pedals.

"Okay. You have both feet on the brake. Can you take your left foot and put on the parking brake? Push it down as hard as you can."

Violet has trouble pressing the parking brake because her legs are shaking so badly, but somehow she does it.

"Now start to relax your leg a little and let's hope the car is stable."

She gingerly relaxes her right leg and the car doesn't move an inch. I hear all four of us sigh in relief. I hear the crunch of a vehicle approaching and I tell the kids to keep her occupied while I wave down the car.

As it rounds the corner I can see it's a big

pickup truck. I wave them down and when they stop I explain to the man and his wife what happened.

"We live a mile from here," the man said as he looked at the car on its perch. "I have an idea. We'll be right back."

He turned around and headed back down the gravel road. About 10 minutes later they reappear with lumber piled in the back of the truck. We lay six 10-foot 4x4 posts side by side across the five-foot gulley, shoving the ends into the rise on the other side. We then lay a large piece of plywood over the posts.

The kids and the man's wife walk to the far side of the deck we made to steady the plywood. We open the door and help the woman out of the car, then we walk her to the road.

She gives me a hug and says, "I don't know how to thank you. I would not have been able to hold on until that truck showed up. You saved me." I can tell she is frail when she hugs me, which makes me feel even more grateful we found her.

We reload the lumber and the couple gives her a ride to their house so she can call family and a tow truck.

When the kids and I get back in the car to continue our journey to town, we are excitedly talking about our adventure.

"You just never know what's around the corner. We were meant to take the shortcut and help that lady."

We finally get to the party and David is already there and so are Sean's friends. The kids have a good time, temporarily forgetting about the nightmare and the rescue we had earlier.

After the party, Sean rides with his dad and Jenn rides with me back to the house.

Soon after the latest incident, we start going to counseling. I have made it clear that our marriage cannot go on this way. The funny thing about it is that every time we walk out of the counselor's office I feel as though we all decided together that it is all my fault. Somehow, David twists things around until I get so confused that I believe that I start the fights and the counselor agrees.

After our latest session, David goes back to work and I head home, it's like a fog lifts and I start to feel angry. It's *not* all my fault…not even close. I can see how I trigger him and I do all I can to change that behavior as we had agreed we would both do.

Finally, after three months of counseling I can see a pattern emerging. I am the bad guy and David is so good at confusing people, he has the counselor (and me) convinced he's right. I realize that he's not going to change — if anything, he's getting worse. He seems to be getting more and more controlling and I can't take it anymore. We have only been married four months, but I feel like I'm in Hell.

One day we are on our way home from picking up Sean in Spokane. We stop at a small gas station so Jennifer can use the restroom. David comes out with a cup of coffee. Once we get on the road, I told him that it triggers me when he doesn't offer to let us get anything.

He gets extremely angry and starts to curse about how he has the right as the driver to get something to keep him awake and he doesn't feel he has to plunk down money on everyone else just because he needs something to stay awake, and I can be sure he will NEVER stop for anything again when others are in the car, he will just keep going, fall asleep at the wheel and crash!

With eyes wide, I tell him that his angry outburst and cursing is out of line. We don't speak the rest of the way home. I feel like I am in trouble again; I have displeased him again. I am also confused. The kids are quiet — too quiet.

We get home and once in bed, he apologizes for being grumpy. I thank him and then explain how I felt confused by his reaction. He gets angry again, repeating everything from the first outburst, and raising his voice. He keeps saying things like, I'm NOT going to buy everyone something every time I want coffee or soda.

I say, "why not? Why can't everyone get something if they want it, why can't you set a spending limit, like a dollar, or fifty cents, or whatever?" His anger keeps rising and we are going around and around, and I finally get out of bed and leave the room to get away from him.

For one, I don't want to be in the room with that toxic behavior; also, he won't lower his voice and our fights bother Jennifer and Sean. I threaten to sleep somewhere else rather than be in the anger.

He comes downstairs and wants to continue the fight, saying he wants me to come back up. Then he threatens me with a comment like, if I want to know what he'll get tired of it's this (not sure what he means by 'this') as he stomps back upstairs. He makes a comment about Jennifer I don't catch, but says it loud enough to wake her (she's right next to our room) and then closes the door loudly.

After I finish calming down, I go upstairs and get into bed. There he goes again! He wants to just make-up, make love, and let it go—pretend like it didn't happen until another time. I don't know how to pretend I'm not feeling hurt, confused, angry, and betrayed.

I feel that he gets triggered, but doesn't want to do the work to understand it. Those are the times he just wants to forget it. It feels like I'm the only one working on my stuff to get clarity and closeness. He just seems to want to throw his temper tantrum and then forget it.

I'm feeling afraid that the marriage is going to turn out like my first one and I'll be left alone in my healing again and have to go my own separate way again in order to be whole.

It's the Fourth of July and we have just finished setting off some spectacular fireworks on the property. The kids are all wound up and running around with sparklers. I smile at them as David and I clean up. He gets that perturbed look on his face again and yells at them to go to bed.

"Let them play a little longer," I say. "They can burn up some of that energy."

As usual, David gets angry. He starts throwing the spent fireworks into the trash can a little too hard and he's stomping all around.

'Here we go,' I think, stressfully.

I get the kids inside and ready for bed and then I go in our room to get ready, too. I keep hoping that by the time he comes back in, David will have calmed down. The kids are in Jenn's room talking when David comes in. He stomps up the stairs, glares at the kids and then stomps into the bedroom and slams the door.

My heart is pounding... I really hate this stress. He starts to yell at me and I just look at him.

"What are you so angry about?"

"I can't believe you undermined me like that in front of the kids!"

"What are you talking about? They were nowhere near us. They didn't hear me."

David storms toward me and slaps me hard in the face. I stumble backwards and fall over the ottoman. I am so dazed I can't think. I scramble up, holding my face and back into the corner by the closet. The door is closed, but the kids hear the *crack* and come flying in. They look in horror at me, and then at David. He starts to yell at them, but Sean screams.

"NO! Don't you touch her again, dad! Back off now!"

David starts to roar at them, but both Sean and Jennifer take a stand in front of me, blocking him from me.

They both start screaming, "Get out! Get out!"

Then Sean says, "Get out, dad, or I'll call the cops!"

David looks incredulously at his son, and then he storms out of the bedroom.

The kids get ice for my poor face while I grab some clothes and pajamas and move into the guest bedroom. It takes an hour for me to get the kids to calm down, and for me to calm down, too.

I get them into bed, thank them, kiss them, and then I head to the guest room. I have no idea where David is, and I don't care. My face is throbbing and I have a headache, neck ache, and my low back hurts from falling over the stool.

I was just dozing off when I hear David knock on the locked door.

"Deb? You in there?" he asks quietly.

"Go away. I am sleeping in here tonight." I didn't dare tell him that I would never sleep next to him again.

"C'mon, Deb. Can't you just get over it now? I'm sorry, I really am."

I don't answer him, but stand against the door as if to keep him out, even though it is locked.

Then he starts to get angry again. "C'mon Deb, don't hold grudges! Come out here now and let's go to bed."

"No, David. Leave me be."

He alternates between whining and fierceness for at least 30 minutes before he finally leaves. I am so shaken and afraid that I actually pull the dresser in front of the door so I can sleep without fear.

The next morning, I drive into town while David is at work and I file for divorce. I can't go on like this and neither can the kids. Everyone is miserable. I guess David made his fear a reality. He made sure we got divorced. I feel very guilty for giving up so soon on the marriage, but I can't let Jennifer learn that this behavior is acceptable.

I am in contact with my folks throughout this process and I learn that dad has been having episodes of vertigo and nausea. After speaking with mom several times in the next few days, I realize my folks need me. Mom doesn't drive and dad can't drive himself when he is ill.

←

Dad has had wanderlust most of his life, primarily due to the way he was treated by his own mom and dad when he was a child. He started taking off and hitchhiking around the country when he was 7 years old. Every time he returned, his mom put him in boarding school or juvenile hall rather than deal with him personally. His dad was never around to deal with his stern wife.

Dad had no safety net—no one who cared enough about him to see his true genius. He searched for it everywhere, but of course he never found it—until he met mom. By this time, however, he was a loner and had no idea how to be a husband and father.

It took years of leaving mom, my two

brothers, and me and then returning again — usually several months later. When he finally stopped running, he learned how to be a family.

As a result of his actions, I went to three elementary schools, two junior highs, and three high schools. This may not seem important, but I have no childhood friends and I never went to any of my proms or reunions.

When Jennifer was born, I promised myself that I would never move her around like that. Through a series of strange turns in my life, I broke that promise several times.

➡

Lisa and Sean are spending the week with their mother in Colville, so I take Jennifer for a walk to tell her about her grandparents.

"I know I promised not to move you around anymore, but we can't stay here and grandma and grandpa need us; they are getting older. I will promise you that we will stay there until you get out of high school."

My understanding daughter looks at me and says, "It's okay, mom. We should go there."

I give her a huge hug. Well, at least we know *where* we are going.

Chapter 13

"What we give our attention to…stays with us. What we let go of…lets go of us." Cat Forsley

When my friends learn of what happened, Diane, Steve, Nan, and Angela show up early one morning with a moving truck. The ladies help me pack and load while Steve keeps an eye on David, who is frantically trying to get to me. The kids are helping and Sean looks miserable.

"I wish my dad hadn't ruined this. I liked having you and Jenn as family."

"Oh sweetie, I'm sorry too. But we will stay in touch and you can come visit whenever you want, ok?"

Sean nods his head and fights back his tears. I hug him for a long time; then the girls and I pile into my car, and Jennifer and Steve get into the truck. We drive away and the dust from the driveway hides David from view.

After spending the night at Diane's, I leave Jenn there to play with her daughter, Hope, while I rent a storage unit in North Spokane and start unloading everything. After about two hours of unloading my stuff, I am getting tired and hungry. Just as I am about to close and lock the storage unit so I can get some lunch, several of my friends show up and start helping me. I am so grateful that I go out and get a couple of pizzas and drinks for everyone.

After another two hours, we are all finished. We are hot, tired, and sweaty from the work, so we all go to the lake and swim, play, and lay on the beach. I will miss these wonderful people when I leave.

We stay at Diane's another three days while I pack up the car and decide on my route to Palm Springs…I couldn't have picked a worse time to head there, since July is miserably hot.

We stay until July 13th so we can celebrate Jenn's birthday on the 12th with our friends. We say our goodbye's after the party and I can see that my trusted friends are as sad to see me leave as I feel.

We take off around 8 a.m. and head east on Interstate 90 toward Montana. We stop in Three Forks, Montana for the night and cool off in the pool before getting dressed for dinner. It is a beautiful summer evening as we walk through town and find a cute place to eat.

The next morning, we set off on Highway 287 heading south to West Yellowstone. We get there in a couple of hours, so we walk around the quaint little town and find a cool little eatery to have lunch. We really like the feel of the town, so we stick around and explore. It's unfortunate we can't go into Yellowstone…we shouldn't take the time or spend the extra money, so I don't suggest it.

It's about three and a half hours to Idaho Falls, where we have a reservation, so we head out around 3:00 to get there by dinner time. Traffic is surprisingly light, considering it's the middle of July; we make great time and get into Idaho Falls about 7:00.

The longest part of our journey is from Idaho Falls to Las Vegas, which is over eight hours, plus the extra time to get through the Salt Lake City traffic. I can't wait to get to Vegas, because that's where my brother lives. He has a thriving post card business and a fine art gallery.

My other older brother, William, is a real character. He is six feet tall, with dark brown hair and hazel eyes. Bill is extremely good looking with a Robin Williams sense of humor. There is no recourse but to laugh until your jaws hurt, especially when he and my brother, Dana, start in together.

Bill is amazing and resilient. It took him years of trying different careers to finally discover that he has a talent for taking phenomenal pictures.

From Hippie in Haight Ashbury with long hair to successful, handsome photographer in only twenty years!

As we near Las Vegas, the temperature

Deborah Alyne Christy

starts creeping up towards 100° and my little red Acura is showing signs of running hot. I take the exit for St. George, a sweet Mormon town, and pull into a service station. I look under the hood and realize the problem immediately — the radiator is very small, so it overheats easily in these hot conditions. I carefully remove the cap and add water; then I buy a gallon of water, since I am still a good two hours away from Vegas, in case I need to add more. It's five o'clock and the temperatures are still above 100°.

"Jenn," I say as I get into the car, "we need to leave the air conditioner off as much as possible so we don't overheat so easily."

"What'll happen if it overheats?"

"It can break the engine and we will be stranded."

"Oh." She responded. "It's okay mom, we can leave it off."

"You are a good girl!"

"I know!"

I giggle at her answer, which makes her laugh. She understands because she is smart and understanding.

Once we were through the canyons separating Utah from Arizona, and Arizona from Nevada, we can see the entire valley and the heat is like a blast furnace. I pull off the freeway and check the radiator. I add more water and then we start the drive to Las Vegas with the air conditioner on full blast.

Chapter 14

"You may have a fresh start at any moment you choose, for this thing that <u>we</u> call 'failure' is not the <u>falling down</u>, but the <u>staying down.</u>" Mary Pickford

We get to Bill's house a little after 7 p.m. and it is still sweltering out. As we walk up to the door, he throws it open and smiles broadly, holding out his arms for us. The first thing I notice is the rush of cold air from the house.

The next day, we go to the gallery and I am blown away by the beauty of his art. Bill goes to help a customer and Jenn is helping Tara, the girl Friday, with stuffing envelopes for his upcoming sale. I wander around, looking at the magnificent works of art. A couple approaches the same picture I'm admiring.

"This is so beautiful. I love this one," sighs the woman.

"I know," I reply with a smile. "I love how he captures the most colors possible. He must wait for everything to be just right. That takes a lot of dedication and patience. Look at the depth of colors. He captured the brilliance of the sunrise as it peeks above the stone and the foreground is still rich with color and not washed out."

The couple nod, smile, and walk toward

Tara. After a few moments, Tara calls for a sales person to help the customers. They purchase the one we were admiring: Awaken, Bryce Canyon.

Bill takes us to lunch and starts talking to me about his postcard line in the desert.

"You need to find work once you get to mom and dad's and I need to find a new sales rep for that territory. Would you be interested in taking it over?"

"Absolutely! But I've never been good at sales. Do you think I can do it?"

"Are you kidding? You just sold one of my pictures for me! I heard you talking to them and you were magnificent."

He tries to give me $100 for selling it and I refuse. "I didn't do it to make money. I'm just happy they bought it."

He keeps trying to persuade me and finally gives up after I won't budge. We talk about the postcards and novelties for the route.

"I'll come down to train you within two weeks so you can get started."

The next morning, Bill buys me three gallon jugs of water and puts them in the back of the car for me. We give him a big hug and then Jennifer and I take off to the folks' house in La Quinta.

I love to take the back roads through the desert—it is away from traffic and people, which is my preference, but I decide to stay on the freeway since my poor car is struggling with the heat. When I stop in Barstow to check the radiator and get some drinks for us, I find a $100 bill sticking out from under one of the water jugs. I smile and shake my head, knowing I have a great family.

We finally get to the house around dinner time and we're starving, since there aren't many gas stations or convenience stores through the desert until you get to Yucca Valley. By then we're only an hour away from La Quinta.

The heat is staggering. A sign says it's still 111° out and it's nearly 5:30. Jenn and I look at each other with wide eyes.

Mom is especially glad to see me because dad has been suffering from his arrhythmia for over 24 hours. I can see the relief in her eyes. Mom doesn't drive, so getting dad to the emergency or the doctor is nearly impossible.

After dinner I talk with dad about it and he is adamant about not going to the ER, so we agree to wait until morning. I step outside around 9:30 and I am shocked that the heat still takes my breath away. It's dark out and yet the temperature must still be in the 90s.

By the time I talk dad into going to the hospital the next morning, it's nearly noon and he is throwing up from the dizziness. We drive to the hospital and they rush him right into the

ER, since we are talking about is his heart. They finally get his heart to convert to a normal sinus rhythm after three hours, so I am able to take him home.

Bill comes down in two weeks like he promised and he takes me around to all his clients and shows me how to restock the postcards and magnets. The route is long, since one of my stops is all the way to Barstow and another is in Ehrenberg, Arizona—opposite directions.

I decide to take the job, so he rents an air conditioned storage unit for me and we go to the old sales rep's home in Palm Springs to get the supplies. We load boxes of post cards, key chains, mouse pads and magnets. Then we load a bunch of postcard racks and signs. By the time we're done, we are hot, sweaty, and exhausted.

Bill takes me to lunch at his favorite Mexican place in Cathedral City and we finally cool off about a half hour later. Next, we go to go to the storage unit and unload everything. He shows me how to assemble the racks and loads one up so I have a sample to go by when I first start working.

Bill heads home two days later, after shadowing me for an entire day to see how I handle everything.

The following week I trade my Acura for a

Deborah Alyne Christy

small Toyota truck with a canopy. I am
embarrassed to say that the dealership really
beat me up on the deal and I didn't feel strong
enough to fight back. I think about my past
lessons with Johanna and I know she would not
be proud of me. Instead of being happy in my
new truck, I am miserable because of the way I
was just treated. Johanna—wow, I haven't
thought about her in so long.

We have been here for about a month, and
tonight I am awakened at 12:30 to my daughter
screaming my name at the top of her lungs. I
jump up and mom is peering from her room,
wide eyed and dad comes down the hall from
the living room. They both ask what's wrong,
and I shrug at them and go into the room.
Jennifer is hysterical, sitting up in bed and
reaching for me. I sit on her bed and hold her
until she calms down.

"Mom, I just had the worst dream ever," she
stammers. She is still shaking like a leaf and
crying.

"Do you want to tell me about it?"

She nods and says, "I dreamed that David
and you were on a bridge and he shot you with a
gun and threw you off the bridge." With that she
began crying harder. "I was so scared."

"Oh sweetie, he can never hurt us again. We
got away from him and now we can have a

normal life here with grandma and grandpa."

Jenn and I have two weeks of walks in the desert, walks in the air conditioned mall, and trips to the movies before school starts. It's nice to spend so much time with my incredible, wise-beyond-her-years daughter. In fact, I have actually learned many things from her.

I learned that it's okay *not to* stay angry after a disagreement with someone you love. It's *okay* to let it go. "After all, we still love each other, right?" Out of the mouths of babes.

I am enjoying the post card job and I find I am actually good at it. I have even been able to acquire new customers. I guess I don't suck at sales after all.

Jennifer seems to be enjoying school, but I notice that her mood is declining for some reason. Christmas break is starting at the end of the week and even though I am worried, I don't push her to share; she doesn't seem ready to talk. So I do what I can; I ask if she wants to talk and I let her know I'm here when she's ready.

Two months pass and Jenn is still not sharing what's bothering her. Her grades are starting to suffer and she still won't tell me why.

I can usually complete my local routes by 3:00, which allows me to be home and available to Jenn. She usually comes in calling our names to see who is around. Today, she bursts through the door wild-eyed and out of breath.

"Jenn! What's wrong?" I say, worried.

"Mom these girls chased me home and they said they'll stick me with a knife if I'm alone."

"What girls; what do you mean?"

"It's a gang, mom. A gang of girls. Maria and her boyfriend Julio are the leaders. Julio keeps trying to kiss me and pinch my butt and now Maria hates me even though I don't like Julio."

"Oh, honey. I am so sorry." I give her a hug and help her with her backpack. "I didn't know there were girl gangs, especially not in middle school."

"There are, mom, there are...and they are mean."

"Okay, Jenn. I am calling the police to see if there is anything they can do to help."

Jennifer looked at me, terrified. "No mom, that will only make it worse for me."

"Honey, they are threatening your life. That's not something I am willing to just wait and see if it gets better."

Jennifer is not convinced and her fear is evident, but I call the police anyway. When they arrive, I ask Jenn to tell them everything. I am shocked, because a lot was happening at school and I knew nothing about any of it.

Kids were sneaking in knives and threatening each other constantly. They targeted the weaker or newer kids to get their compliance and then folded them into their gang. But Jennifer did not play that game and it infuriated them.

The police call the campus police at Jenn's school and it's decided that she will be accompanied to the bus stop by a police cruiser, since I can't be there to take her. After school, dad or I will pick her up at the bus stop. This goes on for several weeks until the boiling point is reached one day at school.

During lunch, Jenn is forced to sit in the campus police office to avoid being harassed. Today, however, there is a disaster preparedness drill. When the alarms go off everyone goes to their designated spots outside for a head count.

Jennifer leaves the office and heads outside to meet her classmates at the meeting point, when she is surrounded by the gang of girls near the exit. The janitor sees the group and tries to get them outside when he realizes they are surrounding a student. He pushes his way through the girls and grabs Jenn's arm. He waves at the gang to get outside for the drill, but they seem more determined than ever to hurt her. Weapons are brandished; Jennifer and the janitor stand back to back trying to fend off the attack, but they are unarmed and outnumbered.

Once outside, the police realize a large group of kids and Jennifer are missing. They run back in and break up the gang, dragging Maria into their office.

The next day Carlos, one of Jenn's classmates, asks her if she has an extra pencil. She gives it to him, but Julio is looking at them venomously. He is convinced that Carlos is hitting on Jenn, so after class he follows Carlos out and beats him unconscious while Maria holds a horrified Jennifer up against a wall. The campus police show up and Julio and Maria are both arrested. Warnings are issued that Jennifer and other kids are to be left alone or attackers will find themselves arrested, too.

The rest of the school year is fairly calm and Jenn seems to be doing better, too, but I can tell she is still not herself. On the last day of school the old gang decides to get even for their friends going to Juvenile Detention. They approach Jennifer and something inside tells her to stand up to them. She focuses on one girl and beats her up, while the others watch in surprise. Jennifer turns, fists raised, and asks who is next. Instead of jumping her, the girls back off.

This gives her a new sense of power; I can see she is no longer afraid and I am proud of her for standing up for herself. I think her summer is going to be much calmer and safe now.

A week after school lets out the principal calls and asks me to come in for a meeting. When I get there, he is looking me up and down as though he is trying to understand my daughter through what he sees of me.

"I'm sorry Mrs. Christy, but Jennifer cannot return to this school in the fall."

"Why is that?"

"She is just too much trouble and she creates problems wherever she goes."

"Excuse me?"

"Yes, since she has been here she has caused many fights. Two students were arrested because of her and now I learned she beat up another student."

I feel my face redden and before I realize it I have risen from my chair, looking at him. He looks as though I might harm him, which really pisses me off. I shake my head in disbelief.

"My daughter was the victim here and I am appalled by your reaction and your perspective on all of this."

He looks at me as though he doesn't understand what I just said. "I have a hard enough time keeping these students in line without your daughter stirring the pot." I suddenly see that this man is afraid of the gangs in his own school.

"Let me make this simple for you, Mr. Castaneda. I agree with you completely. Jennifer has no business being in this school—not as long as you are Principal here. Your apathy and twisted perspective is like a poison; and you poison your school with every breath you take."

I straighten up, feeling disgusted with this man. I look at his bloated face and fat fingers and I can only shake my head at him—I have no words left for this coward. I storm out and get in the car, shaking. I rarely get this angry at anyone, so I am not used to the adrenaline rush I received when facing him.

In August I start checking out local schools to see what options exist for my daughter. After checking out several options I realize that I can't afford a private school. Two weeks before school starts I find a Charter school. I interview the Principal and get a tour around the school. I am impressed; I just wish it wasn't in Indio. Not only is the school a 20 minute drive, but Indio is not always the safest city. Since my choices are limited and time is passing, I decide to register her. Dad has agreed to pick her up on the days I am out of town, so it is doable.

Time passes and Jennifer loves her school. She has made a bunch of friends and, although I am not completely comfortable with it, has a boyfriend. She spends a lot of time with her Charter friends and I can see the difference in her demeanor and attitude—she looks happy. Finally! They hang out at the mall during their Christmas break and I know the mall is safe with plenty of security milling around—especially during Christmas.

Jennifer has only two rules: she cannot leave the mall and she must call either Grandma and Grandpa or me every hour (unless she's at the movies, of course). She is a good kid and I honestly believe she wants to do right, but something is nagging at me and I can't quite put my finger on it.

Christmas break is over in a week Jennifer wants to spend the day at her boyfriend, Jorge's house. I like Jorge; he is a nice kid with good manners. I have never met the rest of his family, however, so I get his number to speak with his mom. I know she and Jennifer have met because she gives Jenn a ride home when she picks up Jorge at the mall.

We talk for several minutes and she seems like a nice person, so I make arrangements to meet her at her house. When Jenn and I arrive at Jorge's, she goes off to be with him and his siblings while Marisol and I talk. Her accent is heavy but her English is fine and we hit it off. She assures me that she will be home all day and the kids won't be alone together. Their house is modest but clean and she agrees to my rules about Jenn and Jorge not going into Indio alone.

We leave after about 30 minutes with a plan for Jenn to return the next day. Jennifer is thrilled and excited, but I still have some reservations. I put them aside and decide to trust my daughter.

It's February now and all has been calm for the last two months...until today. I am waiting at the school to pick up Jennifer, but she is nowhere to be seen. After about 10 minutes I start to get out of the car and I see her emerge from the school, harried and upset. She gets in the car and I can see she has been crying.

"What's wrong, Jenn?"

"Oh mom, Jorge and his family are moving away!" Her eyes well up with tears and her voice is shaky. "They're moving to Albuquerque...in New Mexico!"

"I'm so sorry honey. When are they leaving?"

"In a month! Mom, what am I going to do? I don't want him to go."

"I know it's hard, sweetie. The only thing you can do is spend time with him while he's here."

She looks at me as though I have gone insane. "Mom, you don't understand—I love him!"

I nod and say, "I know you do, and I know it hurts. There is no easy way to deal with this...trust me, I know from experience."

She looks over at me then she turns and looks out her window. Her pain and sorrow are reflected on the window she is facing. I feel so badly for her, but I know she will be okay eventually.

I help her set up as much time with Jorge as possible before they leave at the end of March. There is a dance at school and she wants to go. She makes arrangements to go home with her friend Theresa and spend the night. We head to the school, picking up Jorge on the way. She is happy and excited, but her eyes give her away...I can see how sad she feels, too.

I head home and spend a quiet evening with mom and dad. The next morning, Jennifer calls me to see if she can stay another night. After speaking with Theresa's mom, I tell her it's ok.

Just as I am leaving to pick up Jennifer the next morning, I get a call from Theresa's mom. She probably wants to know what time I am picking up Jennifer. Instead, she is calling to tell me that Jennifer ran away last night and Theresa doesn't know where she went.

I am fighting off panic as I call Jorge's and ask Marisol if Jennifer showed up there. Marisol has not seen her in days. I call all of Jenn's friends and frantically try to find her. It is nearing dusk and I know I need to call the police to get some help finding her. I reach for the phone just as it starts to ring. When I answer, it's Marisol. Jennifer was hiding under Jorge's bed all day and her toddler found Jenn when Jorge was sneaking her some food.

Both relieved and angry, I head out to pick her up. It's a good thing I have to drive 15 miles to Marisol's; it is giving me time to cool down and think. Why would she run away? I get that she loves Jorge, but this is extreme even for a teenager. I can feel that nagging feeling again — the one I brushed away at Christmas break. As I drive, I try to understand that uneasiness. Suddenly, a thought crosses my mind and it feels accurate. I now have a theory as to why she is acting like this.

When I get to the house I am met by Marisol, who is waiting for me in the driveway. She walks with me, apologizing for everything. She can't understand why the kids are acting like this. Jenn appears at the door, her eyes puffy and her face red and blotchy from crying. I feel so badly for her that I can't be angry anymore. We get into the car and drive silently for several minutes.

I start with my theory. Speaking calmly and quietly, I ask her, "Have you and Jorge had sex?"

Jennifer nods and my heart sinks. Jennifer is only 13 years old. "Are you pregnant?"

She shakes her head and I sigh in relief. "When and where did you have sex?"

Speaking just as calmly and quietly, she responds, "In the girls' bathroom at school during the dance." I glance over and she is looking down.

"Then we won't know if you are pregnant for three or four weeks."

Jenn jerked her head up and looked at me. "Oh," is all she said.

It turns out Jennifer is not pregnant, much to our relief. However, she is still having trouble with Jorge's moving, particularly since they are leaving tomorrow. She is further devastated by the fact that she can't spend any time with him because everyone is busy packing and loading the moving van. It's an emotional evening for Jenn and we all hurt for her, too.

Chapter 15

"[A] final comfort that is small, but not cold: The heart is the only broken instrument that works." T.E. Kalem

Time passes slowly for Jennifer and she finds little solace with her friends or school. This morning I go into Jenn's room to wake her for the last day of school, but she is not there. Once again, there is a knot in my stomach and my heart is racing. I call around, but no one has seen her. I call the school, hoping against hope, but she never arrived.

Now I don't know what to do. I drive to the Palm Desert mall and look for her and then I drive around town. I head into Indio next and check everywhere I think she might hide, including Jorge's cousins houses.

I head back home to call the police and report her as a runaway. I hate to do it, but I worry about her safety. Mom comes outside as I pull into the driveway, waving her arms. I start to step out, but she stops me.

"The Greyhound bus depot called. Jennifer was trying to buy a bus ticket to New Mexico!"

"What?! How did they know who she was?"

"The ticket agent could tell she was too

young, so he said he required identification. She showed him her school ID card. Security has her at the depot and they are waiting for you."

I feel at a loss; I have no idea how to help her. I realize as I drive that I need some sort of intervention or assistance. This is even more evident when I see her. She looks miserable. I can see by her posture and expression that she is frightened, too.

I speak with the security guard for a few minutes and then I approach the ticket agent, thanking him for being so observant and for caring enough to stop her. I walk toward Jennifer and she starts to look very anxious. Obviously, she has no idea how I will react.

"Let's go," is all I say to her.

We walk out to the truck and Jennifer looks like she is on her way to the gallows. I can't stand to see her like this, so once in the truck I turn toward her and hold out my arms. She practically leaps into my arms and begins to sob. I hold her for a long time, whispering in her ear that it's safe to let it out and that I love her. Once she stops crying so hard, I release her and say it's time to head home. She nods and straightens up, still crying a little. I start the car and begin the 20 minute drive home.

"Jenn, I love you and I hurt for you; but I am also angry with you. Sneaking off like that and trying to run away was not the answer. You didn't even give me the opportunity to be there for you or to try and help you."

I glance at her and continue. "Do you think that I never felt the way you do? That I never hurt over a boy like you are? I have; and I can be on your side if you let me."

The rest of the drive is silent, other than Jenn's hiccups from crying. As we pull into the driveway, she releases her seat belt and turns to me.

"I'm sorry, mom," is all she says as her eyes well up again.

"I know. Let's go inside. Grandma and grandpa have been worried about you."

The door opens as we walk away from the car and mom looks at her; I can see she wants to be angry with her, but one look at Jenn's face and mom melts. She opens her arms and Jenn falls into her, crying once again.

I drop Jennifer off at school and head into Indio's social services office. The place is full of people and families with noisy kids. I think many of them are migrant workers from the way they are dressed.

I approach the first open window and ask if I can briefly speak with a social worker. The Hispanic woman looks at me dubiously, saying they are very busy now and asking if I am a welfare recipient.

"I can see how busy your are by the amount of people in the waiting room. I am not on welfare and I am not applying for it. I just need a recommendation for a mental health counselor. It's for my daughter. I need help with her behavior."

The woman's entire demeanor changed as she said, "Oh! I can help. I have list of names. Tell me about your daughter."

I explain about Jennifer as briefly as possible, from the sex in the bathroom to yesterday's actions. The woman nods with empathy and then brightens up when I finish.

"I have perfect counselor for you. I know of her well and I think she can help you."

The kind woman gives me a name and phone number, looks at me with sympathy, and wishes me luck with Jennifer. I thank her and walk to the car. I immediately call the counselor on the new cell phone I just bought for my business.

Jennifer has had two months of counseling and I can see an improvement in her mood. I attend some of the sessions with Jennifer, and I also see Callie by myself so she can help me deal with Jennifer's extreme maturity for her age. The problem is that her emotional maturity is *normal* for her age.

It's nearing July and Jennifer has started to get really combative. We are arguing more and I find myself wondering (when it's over), 'who was right—her or me?' And invariably, I find the answer to that question is: we were both right and we were both wrong.

I try to be fair, so when I feel I am wrong, I tell her so. The thoughts that guide me to do this are my need to be honest and my hope that she will learn to be able to admit when she is wrong. But, is my guidance system out of whack? She doesn't seem to be getting it and she definitely doesn't appear to appreciate it.

My daughter shows very little respect for me or for her grandmother these days, mostly through her tone of voice. I try to explain: it's not what you say but how you say it. But, of course, children are deaf at this age.

I tell the counselor on my next solo visit about a conversation where I told my daughter not to continue a behavior and her answer was, "But you do it, too."

"Now," I ask her imploringly, "how do I handle this? She is right, of course. I don't want her to continue the behavior, but I also can't guarantee I'll never do it again."

"You don't have to," the counselor confidently answers.

She goes on to say that my daughter is fourteen and I am her parent. My job is to raise her and teach her. Sometimes I will demand she change a behavior that I possess, and that's okay. She says I have the right as her parent to tell her this is not a democracy for her yet, that she is a child and I am her parent and that's the way it is. Callie says to tell her that everyone — even adults — must answer to somebody.

I go home, armed with this information and I use it against my daughter during our next incident. I feel like a hypocrite. She becomes absolutely hysterical, claiming that if I don't have to do something, then neither does she. Her behavior escalates to name-calling and other assorted terrible things. Okay, *now* it's completely out of hand. I can't let her talk to me like that, and yet a part of me agrees with her.

The fighting continues with a thundering clash of wills. Somehow, we finally call it quits and for the first time in our history, we go to bed so angry with each other that I don't kiss her goodnight and tell her I love her. No matter how angry we have gotten, we have always kissed goodnight. Our pain is immeasurable.

I don't believe in spankings, but sometimes I am so tempted to see if it will help. Then I realize it's only my need to vent my frustration and I never want to vent it physically on another human being.

I cry all the next day, depressed that I feel so ill equipped to handle my career as a parent. I feel as though I'm failing at the most important job I will ever have. For almost every job in the world, we are trained to perform it correctly. But there is no true preparation or training classes for being a parent.

When my daughter returns from a friend's house, she asks why I'm not out working (being self-employed has its advantages). I tell her I am too sad and depressed to face my customers and my tears start to flow again. She looks at me and apologizes for the way she spoke to me and for one of the more hurtful things she said to me. I thank her, still feeling very inadequate.

Over the next couple of days we talk about what happened that night. I ask her what she thinks happened — how it all began. As she talks, I see a pattern emerging. My daughter says or acts in a way that offends me and I tend to jump right into my defensive pose.

I can just see my Hurt-Little-Kid-Self sitting on my shoulder, arms crossed, frowning at this child, and whispering in a sing-song my ear. "How *dare* she talk to us that way… are you going to let her get away with that? Who's the parent anyway? Be careful, if she doesn't respect and fear you, you'll lose control — then you'll have one of those kids you see on the street that scares you."

This time, however, I brush the little me off my shoulder and I listen to her. She is as confused as I am. She sees all of the mixed messages, too. She not only gets these messages from her grandparents and me, but she gets them from school and other parents — basically, every adult seems to be grappling with the issues that surround our families today.

The talking helps because we both understand each other, and hopefully ourselves, a little better. The conclusion I have come to is that there is no real *right way* and no one is ultimately right or wrong.

I tend to lean toward the opinion that children should not be allowed to argue with adults. I have to keep reminding myself that it depends on the situation. If Jenn is trying to get a point across and I am not listening, then who can blame her for wanting to be heard? To argue when I say 'no' after fully listening to her however, is another story.

I have thought a lot about the comment she made when I asked her to stop her behavior. I think that if it's not good for the child, then it's probably not good for the parent, either. However, If it's about an activity (like an R rated movie or alcohol), then I need to explain the legal rules of our society. If it's about behaviors, such as raising my voice to her but not allowing her to raise hers too, then I think there is an imbalance and I need to be willing to abide by the rules as well. After all, I shouldn't be yelling at her, either—it's not a viable way to reach her.

Chapter 16

"Love can sometimes be magic. But magic can sometimes...just be an illusion." Javan

The rest of the year passes fairly easily and before I know it, the Ides of March is upon us with a vengeance. It's already 93° and everyone is wondering if we are in for an unusually hot summer.

It gets steadily warmer and by April 15th, we are at a sweltering 102°! Dad has been outside working in the yard all morning, but even the morning temps are over 80°. I worry about him in the hot weather, since he is going to be 75 years old this year.

Mom and I are sitting at the table talking when dad comes in the back door. We look up at him as he enters the dining room and he is sweating profusely.

"Are you all right, George?" Mom asks.

"No! If I have to live through one more summer here, it will kill me."

Mom retorts, "You say that every year."

"I mean it this time," he pants as he walks toward their bathroom to shower.

Mom and I look at each other and I can see the concern in her eyes. "Maybe it's time to leave the desert."

Without thinking, I let out a "Yippee!" Of course, I then immediately think about Jennifer and my promise not to move her again. I don't say anything to mom, who is already lost in thought about the prospect of moving.

I made friends with the realtor couple who sold Al's and my house, so we give them a call and they come out to look at the property and offer us a selling price.

I pick Jennifer up from school and take her for a drive up the mountain to Idyllwild, where the temps are at least 20° cooler than the desert floor. Jenn tells me about her day as we drive and I tell her about the new clients I picked up this week.

We stop at the dog rescue on the way and visit with the dogs that have been left there. We fall in love with a couple of them, but we know we can't bring one home. Mom and dad's dog, Honey, would never allow another dog in the house. We continue on our drive, talking about all the dogs we saw.

We get into Idyllwild around 4:30 and the temperature is in the low 80s. It feels so good that we walk through the little town and window shop. We go into a small cafe and order sandwiches to take with us and then head over to the park. We sit down at a picnic table and unwrap our sandwiches as I try to figure out how to tell her. When we finish eating, I start to talk about it with her.

"Jenn, I want to talk to you about something that happened today. Grandpa said that the heat is making him sick and he doesn't think he can handle any more summers here."

"Oh no, is he okay?"

"He is right now. But the problem is that I promised you we wouldn't move again until you were out of high school, and now grandma wants to sell the house and move up north."

"What?! *Mom*! I like my school and my friends. I don't want to move!"

"I know, sweetie, but it is out of my hands."

"But you're happy about it, aren't you? You hate it in the desert."

"I'll admit that the idea of moving somewhere cooler appeals to me, but I would have been willing to stay here for you—I told you that when we moved here. Besides, this isn't about me, it's about grandpa."

"I know mom, but I still don't wanna go."

"We can't stay here alone...the whole idea of coming here was to take care of grandma and grandpa. Where they go, I need to go, too. I am so sorry honey."

I watch her and I can see the conflict playing across her face. My heart aches for her. I feel frustrated that we finally get her emotions under control and I have to uproot her again. She is right, though... I am thrilled at the idea of getting out of this heat.

That night in bed, I tried to meditate and speak with Johanna. She has not been with me since I chose to be with David.

"Johanna," I say aloud, "please come to me and help me. I can't quiet my mind right now and I really need you."

Nothing.

"Johanna," I say again, choking back tears, "I really need your guidance. Please help me hear you."

Silence.

I lay there, crying quietly in frustration. How can I help Jennifer if I can't even help myself? How can I grow and help my child heal if I can't hear my guide?

The For Sale sign goes up within a week and the house has a great offer three weeks later. The papers are signed on June 1st with one stipulation: we have to be out of the house by July 3rd.

We pack like mad to get finished on time and the movers arrive on July 2nd to load us up. The new owners show up a day early, trying to hurry us out.

The car is packed by 5:00 but the movers aren't done yet. It starts to drizzle as we give the last of the instructions to the movers before we leave. They are going to store our things until we find a house.

We are planning to stay with my brother, Dana. He lives in a small town just north of Vancouver, Washington. He really wants us to move to Southwestern Washington, but dad and I have our doubts. Neither one of us do well in a place that is cloudy most of the time. After all, we lived in a small town called Orting that is about 20 miles southeast of Tacoma; we know all about the weather there.

←

I started college in Olympia, Washington right after high school, but ran out of money and grants before my winter term in 1975. I had to drop out and get a job, *and* I had to move back home to live with my parents.

The only decent job I could find was graveyard shift at Denny's. I wasn't thrilled with the hours, but the tips were good — especially when the bars closed. The drunken regulars were always very generous. One older regular left me a handful of change. When I picked up the pile of coins, I saw that they were all very old and probably worth money. I asked him about it the next night and he told me to keep them, so I did.

Denny's is where I met Simon, too. Little did I know at the time, but the next few years were going to be the most trying of my life. Simon was enlisted in the Air Force as a corporal. He came in to have breakfast at least three times a week.

Simon was six feet tall and very buff. His reddish auburn hair was cut short for his military job. We flirted for about a month and then he invited me to an enlisted dance on base.

We dated for about eight months, and then decided to get a house together. We rented a small home in Lakewood, not far from the base.

I loved living in Western Washington; it is green and beautiful. The rain and clouds were a problem for me, though — especially in the summer. The most frustrating part was how it would rain all day and then clear up at night so the stars were visible. It was completely backwards! It should have been sunny and warm during the days of summer, with the rain occurring only at night.

Simon had these strange bouts of erratic

behavior where he would start exhibiting grandiose behavior. One day, he was convinced he was Jesus! About three months later, he got in trouble at work for marching up to a Colonel and telling him everything that was wrong with the Air Force and how it needed to be fixed. He was put on Lithium for what the military doctor called manic depression (now known as bipolar) and then given a medical discharge.

One morning we went for a drive to Mt. Rainier for the day. We drove through the tiny town of Ashford and stopped at an art community to browse the different little outdoor shops, where I bought a piece of shale on which the artist painted a basket of flowers. We stopped at a quaint restaurant called the Copper Creek Inn, about two miles from the entrance to Mt. Rainier. The lunch was excellent. We had soup and a homemade mini bread loaf. And then we had the best blackberry pie I have ever tasted.

We decided to take a walk before heading back, since it was too late to go into the park. We walked through the back of the café and into the woods. We were surprised to see small cabins scattered around the other side of the creek.

We walked back down and crossed the creek at the highway. There was a small group of four cabins to the left and three cabins along the creek, separated by forest on either side of each cabin. The first cabin had a couple sitting on the little porch, and we approached them. Their names were Summer and Elijah Blue. They were the caretakers of the property.

Through them we found out that the owner's mom lived in the second cabin, but it was empty since she died. The lodge has been empty since the new owners took over in 1975.

Summer looked at us and then said, "The back cabin is for rent, and it is empty and unlocked, so feel free to go inside."

The cabin was very rustic and small, with a small bedroom and bathroom, and a large open area for the kitchen, dining, and living rooms. There was an propane heater in the bedroom room and a wood cook stove for heat and cooking in the main room.

It was sparse and small and plain, and I *loved* it. I always knew I was a country girl at heart, but this was the first time I actually felt it. As we walked back toward the road holding hands, we saw the caretakers were still sitting outside.

Simon walked us over to them and asked how much the cabin rented for and we were shocked to hear it was only $85 a month.

We headed home, replete, peaceful, and lost in thought. As we pulled into the driveway, all that lovely warmth and peace was shattered. Someone broke our bedroom window and robbed us. Between the shock, fear, and anger was confusion. We didn't have anything of value. An old stereo, an old TV, and some of my inexpensive jewelry are all they got. The records, which they didn't touch, would have probably been worth more than what they stole.

We both felt disturbed at the stolen property as well as the stolen sense of safety. Neither of us wanted to stay in the neighborhood any longer, so we boarded up the window and the next morning we headed back to Mt. Rainier and took the cabin in the woods.

➡

We stop for dinner on the way out of town and poor Jennifer is absolutely miserable. I have never seen her look so sad and lost — not since Jorge.

We decide to head up highway 395, going up through the Lucerne Valley to Victorville to avoid going through Riverside County and all the traffic. We stay the night in Lone Pine and head back out after a late breakfast.

We make a pit stop and get a snack in Topaz Lake, just over the Nevada border; then we head on to Reno, where we have reservations at Circus Circus. The room is bright and large, with two queen beds and a little refrigerator.

I am hoping this stay will help Jenn's mood and help her find a little joy. Mom and dad go downstairs to play the slot machines and I leave Jennifer in the room watching TV while I go check out the arcade.

When I return, mom is in the shower and Jennifer is jumping on the bed. She is so surprised to see me that she jumps too hard and hits her head on the ceiling. She flops down on her butt and looks at me, eyes wide but a bit of a grin lingering on her lips. It is so good to see a smile that I can't be angry.

"Jenn!" I exclaim.

Then before I know it we are both laughing. It's so good to hear her laugh. I walk over and give her a hug, then gently admonish her while we are both still giggling.

The four of us go to the buffet for dinner, then I take Jennifer down to the arcade and we have a great time for nearly three hours.

The next morning after we all have breakfast, Jenn and I head back to the room and mom and dad go off to play the slots. We are staying another night, so I take a bath while Jenn watches TV.

We get to Dana's house two days later. I start looking for houses in the area, since mom and Dana want us to live on this side of the mountains. He introduces me to a realtor friend of his and we go off every day and look at several houses. Most of them are out of our price range and none of them are right for us.

Jenn's dad is traveling to Canada on vacation, so he stops by Dana's and takes Jennifer with him for two weeks. That should help get her mind off things for a while.

Tanya and I spend over a week looking at houses and there is only one that I take the folks to see. It was built in the 1960s and it has only two bedrooms; but it backs up to a nature preserve and has nearly ¼ acre, so there is room for expansion. The only drawback is the price. There would be no money for an extra bedroom.

We finally discuss looking in North Idaho, which is my preference. I take off for two weeks and stay with my friend, Diane. I meet with a friend of mine, Kelly, who is a realtor.

I spend a week driving by properties that Kelly has found and when I have six or so, he and I look at them. This goes on most of the summer, and whenever I have at least six potential homes, I go back to Dana's and pick up Jenn and the folks, and drive them over to see the properties. We always stay at the Hamptons in Spokane Valley, so whenever we arrive they give us a warm welcome.

It's August and we still haven't found the

right place, so we decide to stay at the Hamptons until we find a place. We want to get settled before Jennifer has to start school.

Finally, we find the perfect house two weeks before the start of school. It has a finished basement with two bedrooms and a full bathroom, so it's like Jenn and I have our own place to watch movies, play games, and just be together. The best part is that it is only a four block walk to the high school.

I get a great job at one of the local businesses, Coldwater Creek. I am so happy. The people are wonderful and there is a family atmosphere about the place. The best part is I am only ½ mile from Jenn's school and a mile from home.

I've been thinking about David and the reasons I attracted the experience of being with him. Obviously, I brought him into my life for a reason. Perhaps I was just too blind to see the signs that a relationship with him was all wrong. I guess the old saying, "Love is blind," can be true.

Johanna never came to me the whole time I was with David and it's been nearly two years since I have been able to hear the voices of my guides again. At the time, I was certain I had been abandoned.

I took a long bath last week and was

delighted when I was finally able to meditate. I asked Johanna why she hadn't warned me of the poor match David and I made.

She smiled at me with mild surprise and replied, "I did warn you — often. But you were so intent on the experience that I stepped back and allowed you to have your reality.

I look at her, puzzled.

"Did you not have intuitions that the relationship was not in your best interest? Did you not have headaches? You chose not to listen. You chose to ignore your inner voice and follow your mind. Your conscious mind is very good at talking you into things, is it not? It uses emotions, such as being in love or guilt to sway your better judgment. Learn to listen to your inner guidance. Learn to listen *less* to your emotional responses."

"That was you? You are the little nagging voice I hear?"

Johanna laughed out loud. "So, you hear me as a nagging voice?"

I felt my face flush as I tried to recant, which made her laugh even more. "I never realized that I could hear your voice, too…I mean, when I am not meditating."

"How else do you think I can be heard when you refuse to meditate?"

"I don't refuse to meditate, Johanna. There

are times I can't quiet my mind enough to get relaxed. I try filling with white light, just to find myself on some train of thought and five minutes has passed."

"And you do not feel like you can control it?"

"I *can't* control it, that's the point. As soon as I catch myself on a thought, I release it and continue filling with light, just to find I've been gone again. There comes a point when I have to let it go so I can wash up and get out of the tub."

"Do you know why this happens?"

"I assume it's because some part of me doesn't want to change or take responsibility for my problems."

"That is good. What else?"

"Ummm…well, if I take responsibility then I have to take some action to change. And change is hard."

"The only reason change can be hard is because the human mind wants and needs to feel it is in the right. Taking responsibility is admitting you created a life experience that wasn't good for you, which makes your mind and its decision-making ability wrong. Your mind does not like to be wrong. So it hides painful memories and releases chemicals that take you into a heightened state of stress. Now you are so busy dealing with the stress that you cannot think about change."

"How do I circumvent my mind?"

"It is more about understanding your mind. It is about loving your mind. When you fight with yourself because you can't meditate or do something important to you, then you create even more chaos.

"Think about how you talk to yourself when you do something wrong. What do you say to yourself?"

"I say something like: what's wrong with me? Why can't I do this? Or I'll put myself down because I know better, like: I am being so stupid! Why do I keep doing that?"

"Correct. Do those thoughts bring peace or stress?"

"Stress. Because it tends to just get worse...like a never-ending cycle of abusive behavior."

"Ahhh. Did you hear what you just said?"

"Yes! Oh my gosh, I never realized that I still treat myself in an abusive manner."

"It is one of the untruths that you decided to keep. You will need to be aware of the times you treat yourself abusively. Think about it for a moment. Would you speak to your worst enemy the way you sometimes speak to yourself?"

"No. NO! I wouldn't!"

"Then what you need to discover now is

why you are so cruel to yourself. Why you beat yourself up so badly. I will leave you with these thoughts, dear one. Be at peace."

"Thank you, Johanna."

Wow, I still have a lot I don't see.

Chapter 17

"The young always have the same problem--how to rebel and conform at the same time. They have now solved this by defying their parents and copying one another."
Quentin Crisp

The year passes fairly calmly and it's April before I know it. Jenn spent her spring break with friends at the mall and at the local arcade during the day.

Jenn's been back in school for two weeks now and something is definitely off. My dad thinks she is stealing money from him, but can't prove it. Her behavior is changing, too. She's more erratic than usual. Twice in the last week she was gone when I went to look for her, showing back up two or three hours later with some excuse about popping over to a friend's house, ignoring that she didn't ask or let us know.

She has been more argumentative, too…especially to her grandma. I know it can be hard on her here, since our home is not mom, dad, and kid—it's mom, kid, grandma, and grandpa. Having one mother in the house is hard enough for any teenager, but having two must be like torture. I try to be understanding, but she seems to be getting worse every day.

Then, in May I get a call from Jenn's school. She has been caught getting high on pills with her best friend, April. When I arrive at the school, Jennifer is highly agitated and involuntarily shaking her legs up and down.

It turns out that kids are turning to over the counter drugs to get high. In this case, it is Coricidin Cough and Cold; the kids call it triple C. The principal suspends her for the rest of the week. He gives me her books and assignments for the week and I take her home, unsure how to proceed.

We get downstairs and Jennifer sits on the couch, shaking her legs and patting her thighs. I just look at her.

"Mom, don't worry. I won't ever do this again. I hate this feeling."

"I'm glad, because taking that much cold medicine can hurt with your liver. It's dangerous, Jennifer."

"I know, mom, I get it — really."

"Okay. You are grounded until you go back to school next week."

"Okay mom, I understand."

Jennifer is on her best behavior the rest of the school year (two weeks), but she still seems off to me. I need to figure out what is going on.

Summer is nearly over and Jennifer's

behavior has been all over the map and I still can't figure out what's going on. But she hasn't broken any rules or snuck out, so I feel that maybe we can get the behavior under control, too.

Dad and I have a date on Sunday evenings to watch a movie together. Jenn doesn't want to watch with us or with grandma, so she stays downstairs to watch our TV.

After the movie I go downstairs and Jennifer is already in bed. I head to bed, too.

The next morning, I go in to wake Jennifer for school, but she's not there. What I thought was Jennifer in bed is actually pillows and clothes. Now what? I go upstairs and there's no sign of her anywhere. (not like I expected to find her, but hope *does* spring eternal, doesn't it?)

I go into the kitchen and look outside, lost in thought. There's a strange car in front of the house and as I look at it I can see Jennifer starting to get out. I completely lose it. I stomp outside, look to see who is in the car, grab her arm, and drag her into the house and down the stairs. She looks like she just woke up.

"Whose car was that?!" I shout. "Where have you been?"

"Mom, calm down!"

"*Excuse* me? You don't get to tell me to calm down. I want answers and I want them now."

"That was Jacob's car, a boy I like." She looks at my face and hurriedly says, "We didn't do anything, mom. I snuck out to hang with my friends and Jacob drove me home. But I couldn't get in. Grandpa had already locked the door for the night, so I slept here in Jacob's car."

I have to be at work soon, so I inform her that she is grounded again. "You will spend the day cleaning the downstairs until it shines."

Jennifer literally starts to freak out. She lashes out at me, screaming like a mad person. I grab her by her ponytail and hold her head down until she calms down, which takes nearly 10 minutes. I push her onto the couch and tell her to stay there until I get ready for work.

I give her a list of chores that I expect to be completed and head upstairs to leave, when the doorbell rings. I open the door to find two police officers standing there.

"Can I help you?" I ask, confused.

"We got a report of child abuse at this address."

"What?" is all I can muster when mom and dad also come to the door to see what's happening.

"Who called you?" asks my mom.

"Jennifer Christy."

Mom, dad, and I just look from one to the other, each with a bemused stare.

"I'll go get her," I say.

"I will go, ma'am. Where is she?" I point toward the stairs and the older policeman heads down to talk with Jennifer.

The other policeman interviews the three of us in the living room. We tell him all about her actions and behavior over the last month or two.

Jennifer comes up the stairs with the policeman and he points her to the living room as he and the other policeman go into the kitchen and talk. Jennifer sulks in the corner of the room, not looking at any of us.

The older policeman asks to see me while the other one goes to speak to Jennifer. He has a rugged, kind face and he looks at me with sympathy. I ask him what else I can do to help her get her life straightened out.

"There is a behavioral health clinic for children in town. I suggest you talk to them. In the meantime, I warned her about calling 911 for no reason and Officer Petrie is admonishing her as well."

I thank them for their time, close the door, and then turn to Jennifer. She looks sheepishly at me and gives me a weak apology. She agrees to do the chores without a fight, so I tell her that we will see how the next few days goes before I let her be with her friends.

School starts three weeks later and I am so concerned for my daughter's behavior that I can hardly focus on anything.

I get a call at work from the police in October, saying that my daughter is being held in the security office at Target for shoplifting. With a heavy sigh, I leave for my lunch break and head for Target.

I step into a tiny room with security monitors covering three of the four walls. It turns out that Jennifer was caught trying to steal triple C. They agree to let her leave in my custody with no charges pressed, since it was her first offense.

I take Jennifer home, call Lake City Behavioral Health, and make arrangements to meet with a counselor Saturday morning at the hospital's ER.

The counselor asks Jennifer and me dozens of questions, then agrees that Jennifer will benefit from their in-patient program. I look at Jenn at the realization she will have to stay there and she gives me a slight nod, yet looks a little worried. I agree, but I have many reservations. She is only 15 and still my little girl, even with all the problems.

Jennifer stays in LCBH for six weeks. She

seems fine every time we have a family meeting, yet when I meet with the psychiatrist, Dr. Chandler, alone he tells me all the things she is doing that keeps her there.

Apparently, she has started mirroring other kids and taking their problems as her own. For example, there is a boy there who is suicidal and Jenn announces she is suicidal, too. If a child claims to be suicidal, then they cannot leave the program — even if the counselors know it is not true.

After eight weeks, they finally decide Jennifer is ready to come home. I arrive and a female counselor brings in Jenn after I spend about 20 minutes with the doctor. We all talk for a few minutes and the counselor makes a comment about bringing her back if there are any problems. Jennifer freaks out and begs me not to bring her back. Before I can even respond, Dr. Chandler threatens her.

"If this is how you are going to act, perhaps we should keep you a little longer."

"Noooooooo," is all Jennifer can say as she moves to the corner of the room and cowers in absolute terror.

"That's it," says Dr. Chandler, "call a code gray and take her back into the clinic."

"Wait," I say, "what's a code gray?"

"It's when a patient is not cooperating. We

put her into solitary confinement for up to 48 hours, depending on her behavior."

Jennifer cowers even more and covers her head with her arms as though she is trying to disappear as the counselor grabs her arm and roughly pulls her to her feet.

"**Leave her alone!**" I yell at the counselor as I leap up and knock her hand from Jenn's arm.

Jennifer instantly goes back down into the corner. I have never seen Jennifer cower to anyone. If anything, she tends to confront authority figures. I am truly confused and concerned.

Dr. Chandler stands and faces me. "This is not acceptable behavior from either of you! She cannot be allowed to disregard our rules. She needs to go back into the clinic *right now*."

"You will not *touch* her. She will *not* return to the clinic. I want her belongings her in *five minutes*, do you understand?"

The doctor nods to the counselor, who disappears through the intake door. I stand in front of Jennifer the entire time, staring down Dr. Chandler. Within minutes she reappears with Jenn's things in a black plastic bag.

I take Jenn's hand a stand her up beside me. I take the bag and we walk hand-in-hand out the door. As soon as she hits the freedom of the parking lot, she breaks down.

"Thank you, mom for not leaving me there!" Jennifer manages to say as she sobs into my shoulder.

In that moment I wonder if I did the right thing by taking her there. I hold her for a long time, then pour her into the car so we can go home. Once I got Jenn home and everyone hugged and talked and laughed and cried, I got settled into a hot bubble bath with candles.

This whole thing brings back unpleasant memories of my own past.

←

Simon and I moved to Ashford April 28th, 1976 and rented the cabin. I felt a freedom I had never experienced before. I got a job at the Copper Creek Inn as a waitress and Simon took on small carpentry jobs around the area.

Our cabin was small with a wood cook stove/oven close to the front door and a small space called a kitchen beyond. The woodstove warmed the large room, which also included the living room and dining area. Our little bedroom had an old iron bed with lots of blankets, and a small built-in propane heater.

Every morning one of us had to jump out of bed, turn on the heater, and jump back into bed and wait for the room to warm up enough to get up.

It was nearing October and the fall air was crisp and clean. We discussed what needed to be done before winter settled in, but Simon was acting erratic again, and it was hard to get him to focus for very long.

One morning, we had a fight over nothing and he became so enraged that he grabbed me by my throat and lifted me off the ground, pushing me into the side of the shower. He was choking me and I was close to losing consciousness when I saw a look of horror flash across his face. He released me immediately and I slid to the floor.

He kept stuttering an apology, then he turned and rushed out the door. I heard him drive away as I was struggling to my feet.

I grabbed my clothes and personal items, shoved them into my car, and drove off the mountain and away from my dream of living in the country.

I decided that I wanted to be closer to the ocean, so I drove west. I had no idea where I was going or what I was going to do once I got there. I stayed on Highway 12 until I got to Aberdeen, then I headed south on the 101. I figured I would wait until I found a seaside town and then stop.

I pulled into a small town called Raymond

for some hot coffee and a meal. I went into a coffee shop that belonged to the hotel above it. I was having a conversation with the owner while I ate at the counter. For some reason, I told him everything.

He watched me sympathetically and then offered me a job.

"I know Raymond isn't on the beach, but it is a nice town and I need a waitress. The job includes room and board in the hotel." He pointed up as he said it.

I had no other options at that point, so I said yes.

I had been working there for several weeks when I began feeling despondent and lost. I had spoken to mom a few times and she told me Simon had moved into their little town, Orting, after I left.

One night I decided it was all too much, so I went to the coffee shop staff in their rooms and bummed pain pills and valium from each of them. I made a screwdriver and downed the pills. I called Simon to say goodbye, knowing he was too far away to help me in time.

I went to my room and waited for the inevitable. I was barely aware of the commotion outside my door or the way Simon burst through it. He dragged me to my feet and ordered the owner to get coffee. Simon walked my limp body up and down the hallway and forced me to drink the coffee. He had my coworkers gather my things, then he took me downstairs and poured me into my car. He drove away, leaving his truck in Raymond for the time being.

I kept muttering about wanting to see the ocean, so he found a nice beach outside of Aberdeen and parked. I was still very weak from all of the drugs in my system, so I stayed in the car for a while.

Simon started talking with another man as I was working my way out of the car. I walked to the water and just kept walking into the ocean. The cold water caused me to shake uncontrollably and I passed out. The next thing I knew I was waking up on the sand to Simon leaning over me soaking wet and roughly rubbing my arms, chest, and stomach.

The young man offered to let us go to his house to warm up, so I took a hot bath while he and Simon got our clothes clean and dried.

Once Simon got me back to his house in Orting, it was after midnight. I didn't want to be there with him, so I kept trying to leave the house until finally Simon snapped. He grabbed my suitcase and flung it out the door. The zipper broke on impact and my clothes were strewn all over the lawn. I ran out and started throwing my clothes back into the suitcase when I found some caffeine pills I had. It was the only drug left to me, so I took a handful and began walking down the street. I was crying uncontrollably and had no idea what to do.

It was too late to go to mom and dad's, so I just walked until dawn. When I finally arrived back at Simon's, he ran out to meet me and was visibly worried about me.

"I need help, Simon," I cried.

"I know. Let's get you to the hospital."

I wasn't sure what they could do, but I said yes anyway. I was out of control and I knew it.

When we arrived at the hospital in Puyallup, they said they were not equipped to handle mental patients and gave us the names of two hospitals in Tacoma.

We went to the first one and they put me into an ER room while Simon and the staff talked. When the doctor arrived I had fallen asleep. He looked at Simon and said to take me home — truly depressed people don't fall asleep that easily. Even once Simon described the last 12 hours to him, we were turned away.

The next hospital on the list was St. Joseph. When we got there, I made sure to stay awake. When Simon and the ER nurse entered, I began to cry.

"Please don't send me away."

"I won't, honey. I'm sorry about what happened at the other hospital. We are going to take care of you, okay?"

I nodded gratefully.

I spent nearly a month there while they tried different meds on me. I saw a very strange psychiatric doctor who had me on three different tri-cyclic drugs and he was also giving me injections of antidepressants and B vitamins.

My folks didn't like the way I was so out of it when they visited, but the doctor was adamant about my meds. They were instrumental in getting me out of there even though I was 20 years old at the time. Mom really didn't like the doctor and she helped me find someone else who was also closer to home.

The new doctor took me off all of those antidepressants and replaced them with one pill a day. I never fully got over the depression and had to learn how to live with it — without doing myself in accidentally or deliberately.

Chapter 18

"You may not realize it when it happens, but a kick in the teeth may be the best thing in the world for you." Walt Disney

I hope things will improve now, especially after the harrowing experience Jennifer had at LCBH. Things don't always go the way I hope—particularly when my daughter is involved.

At first, Jennifer is participating in her recovery. She genuinely seems to want to get better. Things begin to erode within three months.

In January, Jennifer starts sneaking out of the house by climbing out of her bedroom window and up the window well.

In February, Jennifer is suspended from school and arrested for bringing a razor utility knife to school in order to threaten a classmate. She spends a week in juvenile detention. We now have family counseling at the house, mandated by the court. Jennifer also has a Psychiatrist who dispenses her meds and counsels her.

March through April, Jennifer sneaks out of the house in the middle of the night. It gets so bad that I have to call the police several times to try and find her.

In May, she is expelled and arrested for beating up a girl in school.

Jennifer gets a local job in June at a fast food restaurant, where she is fired for stealing. She gets another job that she loses because she ends up in Juvie again over stealing triple C. She gets out and gets another job that she loses for stealing money.

In August, Jennifer runs away from home. Dana is visiting for a couple of days, and we go looking for her at the Fair twice. I call all of her friends, but no one is giving any information. I call her best friend, Tommy, and he finally tells her that he's going to tell me where she is if she doesn't go home.

After being gone for a week, Jennifer is caught and arrested. She spends two weeks in Juvenile Detention and then comes home in time to start school.

I give my two weeks' notice at Coldwater Creek due to Jennifer, my need for foot surgery, and my parents' health issues.

I work from home doing freelance tech writing while completing an online Real Estate course.

Jennifer has a friend that I really like. Her name is Erica and she has come to stay with us from time to time when her parents kick her out. This September, she comes over for a visit and she looks really beat up. When I ask her what happened, she says that her dad through her down the stairs because he was pissed at her.

I am very alarmed and tell her that I want to turn him in, but she freaks out and runs off. Jennifer tells me they are tweakers (people who do meth) and very strange. She begs me to drop it. I don't know what to do, and then Erica comes back to the house and asks me to stay out of it. She is afraid of them. The police were called when they hurt her older sister, but nothing came of it and her parents punished her severely.

I drop it, against my better judgment, because of the intensity of Erica's insistence that it will make life worse for her at home.

The high school starts a fund raising drive selling chocolate in October. Jennifer and Erica go out after school every day and collect names and money for delivery in November.

About a week into the drive, there is a knock on the front door while Jennifer is at school. When I open the door, two police officers are there. They have come to inform me that Jennifer has been arrested for forging checks that people have given her for the drive.

One of the officers, who has been to the house at least twice before, tells me she has graduated to a felony and it is very serious.

"Her arraignment is tomorrow. You can call the court to find out the information." He shakes his head, slowly, and says, "I'm really sorry Mrs. Christy, I know how hard you have been trying to help her."

I thank him as they leave, and close the door. I call Juvenile Detention and I am informed I cannot see her until her arraignment tomorrow at 3:30.

Jennifer's dad, Al, flies up from California to offer moral support. We arrive at the court, find her courtroom, and head in. We sit on the bench in the front of the room and wait nervously.

A door opens at the far left side of the courtroom and five kids in orange jumpsuits shuffle into view. They are chained together, with chains on each of their ankles. Their arm chains are fastened at their wrists and wrap around their waist, keeping their hands in front of them.

When Jennifer comes into view, we both gasp. It is so hard to see her trussed up like this. Al and I hold hands to steel ourselves against the emotions, both of us almost in tears.

The kids sit in the jury seats and are brought to the Defense table one at a time. Jennifer is the third one, and we hold our breath as she shuffles to the table directly in front of us.

She is looking down as she tries to walk with chains clamped to her legs. She sneaks a look at us as she approaches, but quickly looks down again, turns, and sits in the chair with the help of the bailiff.

The judge looks over her papers quietly for several minutes, looks up at her for several seconds, and then continues to read.

"You have been in my court quite a few times, Miss Christy. I see the most recent one is just last February for bringing a razor knife to school. I remember you; and I think I may owe you an apology.

"I recall now that back in February my instincts told me that I should have committed you to the state for restitution and rehabilitation. But your probation officer at the time disagreed and fought for you. I also see that your mother said she would be willing to give you another chance.

"If I had committed you back then, you would have been there nearly a year by now. If you complied with the rules and showed change, you could have been out by your birthday next July. If I commit you today, you will be there until you are 18 ½. All that's left now is to speak with your current probation officer and your parents. Mrs. Gill, would you like to start?"

Jennifer's probation officer stood and began recanting the offenses, referring to papers that were then given to the judge.

⬅

I was nervous when Jennifer's probation officer, Mrs. Kylie, was promoted last March because it meant getting a new PO up to date. It was stressful to begin with, so having to relive it again by filling in a new person sounded like torture.

When I met Mrs. Gill, my fears were assuaged. She was thoroughly briefed by Mrs. Kylie and she read everything herself, too. I remember our first meeting together, because she really caught me off balance. She came to the house, and after seeing our home and having a conversation with my folks, she sat me down to talk. She interviewed me for about 30 minutes, asking mostly personal questions.

"Mrs. Christy, I have gone over all of

Jennifer's paperwork and I have interviewed her at length at the detention center. I can tell that she is a master manipulator by the way her previous PO and counselors have reacted to her. After speaking with you I am convinced that the purpose of her negative comments about you and her grandparents is to deflect her true nature and behavior.

"She must be a very good liar because she has had her teachers, counselors, and probation officer completely on her side."

"Unfortunately, she is a believable liar," I responded.

➡

The judge's voice brings me back to the courtroom as he says, "I would like to hear from Mrs. Christy now."

I stand up shakily as Jennifer glances back at me with a pitiful, apologetic face. "Your Honor, I have tried everything to help my daughter, from time in NIBH to counseling and medications. No matter what I try, she seems determined to stay on this destructive path. I am afraid for her safety. I can't keep her from sneaking out in the middle of the night, so I never know if she is alive and safe or if she has overdosed on triple C or been raped… or worse.

"Jennifer's father has come from California to be here for us. I don't know if he wants to share or not," I say as I motion his way.

"Mr. Christy, do you have anything to add?"

Al stands as I sit back down. "I know Deborah has tried everything in her power to help our daughter. I trust her decisions."

As he sits back down, Jennifer looks back at me...if looks could kill, I'd be dead. I knew she would be angry, but that look was pure rage.

The judge paused as he sized up Jennifer, then he looked over the records and past rulings and made his decision.

"Jennifer Rebecca Christy, you are removed from your mother's custody and remanded to the State of Idaho. You will be transported to St. Anthony, Idaho where you will remain *at least* until 6 months after your 18th birthday. This facility is a lock-down with heightened security. I am sending you to St. Anthony because of your history of running away.

"Once released, you will be transferred to a group living facility in Boise where you will be taught life skills.

"You will appear before this court again when you have successfully been employed at the same location for 6 months, opened and maintained a checking account since employment, found a place to live, stayed off drugs and alcohol, and observed the law.

"At that time I will decide whether your case is closed or you continue probation with random drug testing."

The judge bangs the gavel, which makes me jump. The bailiff walks Jennifer to one of the detention officers, who guides her out the same door she entered. The bailiff is calling the next child's name as Al and I stand. I glance at the judge, who gives me a slight nod. I nod back as I turn to leave, trying not to cry.

We go see Jennifer at the detention center a couple of hours later. I am so nervous…what do I say to her? How do I help her adjust and prosper at this facility? How do I hide my relief? How do I hide my fear that I have lost custody of my child?

Once we enter the room where Jennifer is waiting, all of my questions fly right out of my mind…she is obviously really angry with me.

"Hi honey," I begin as I ignore her face. "Do you know when they are transferring you or how long we have before you leave?"

"No, mom. It's a secret. No one knows when we leave."

"Why is that?" Her dad asks.

Jennifer shrugs and says, "Something about not telling the family so they can't try and stop it."

"Oh."

We sit in silence for a few moments, then Jennifer turns to me. "Mom. Why didn't you fight for me?"

"I *did* fight for you."

"I just wanted one more chance."

"I know you don't realize it because you spent a few days to a couple of weeks in detention here and there every time you broke the law — but you have been in jail 22 times in two years. How many one-more-chances do you want?"

"I just wanted one more." She spews out in anger.

I raise my voice slightly and say, "Jennifer, this *is* your one more chance. If you don't get it at St. Anthony, then you will never get it; and you will end up with a life like you have now — or dead."

Jennifer shook her head in anger and went silent. Al tried to talk to her, but her answers were curt and unkind.

"I'm flying home tomorrow. Is this how you want to spend you last few hours with us? I don't know when I will see you again."

"Sorry dad, I'm just too mad now."

"Okay."

We stand up to leave, but Jennifer stays in her chair, looking out the window and ignoring us. As we step outside, I burst into tears. There are so many emotions playing in my head that I am overwhelmed.

Al holds me and then walks me to the car. He opens the door to his rental car and helps me in. We go to the house to try and explain everything to mom and dad.

I receive a call the next day from Mrs. Gill, explaining that Jennifer was spirited away in the middle of the night to begin her journey to St. Anthony. They will stop in Caldwell, where Jennifer will stay for up to two weeks while they wean her off her meds. She will then be counseled and evaluated to see if she can remain off of them. Once a decision is made, she will continue her journey to St. Anthony.

Starting next week, I will be part of a weekly conference call with Mrs. Gill and various staff at the detention center to discuss Jennifer. The first call will include her physician and mental health doctor. I'm sure we will be discussing how she's coping as her meds are reduced in stages until she is off them.

Al heads back to his motel and I try to quiet my mind, but I simply cannot. I have always had the best luck meditating while taking a bath so I start the water, pour in my favorite bubble bath, light the candles, and get in.

I let out a huge sigh as I sink down into the

fragrant water. I close my eyes and start gathering the white light around me. Every time I start to breathe the light, my mind flips to a thought. Sometimes, it takes awhile to recognize that I've been derailed.

After 20 frustrating minutes, I give up trying to bring in the light. I decide to let the light just pour over me like a waterfall, but Jennifer's face and her orange jumpsuit crash into my thoughts.

"FINE!" I yell so loud that I flinch, which causes water to slip over the edge of the tub.

Thanksgiving is only three weeks away…how on earth will *that* go? The first few weeks are a dazed blur. I mechanically go through my day, not remembering at the end of it what I actually did. There is a flash of relief from time to time that Jennifer is not here, which is immediately followed by intense guilt.

The only thing I really remember clearly is that whenever I go into a store and see a pregnant woman or one with a baby, I quickly and spontaneously think, "You poor thing. You have no idea what's coming."

It's been 10 months since Jennifer left Coeur d'Alene. Summer has nearly lost to the advancing fall and there is probably about two weeks left of the perfect, high 70s weather that we have in mid-September.

I finally get to go see her! She has progressed enough to enjoy privileges, like visitors and gifts from home. The gifts were usually things like their own shampoo, lotion, deodorant, and other everyday needs.

The timing is perfect, too. I have just enough time to go before there is any threat of snow. St. Anthony is South of West Yellowstone and directly West of the Grand Tetons.

It's a long drive from here to St. Anthony, so I'll be gone at least five days. I decide to drive as far as I can and stop when I find a nice town to stay the night. Since school is back in session, I am certain to have no trouble finding lodging on the long trek through Montana.

I make it to the quaint town of West Yellowstone by 4:00 and find local lodging. After I drop my bags inside the room, I grab my light jacket and head back out the door. It's still warm outside — in fact, it's a perfect fall day — so I tie my jacket around my waist and start walking toward the touristy downtown area.

I browse through the myriad of shops, fascinated by the diversity. Money is tight, so I have $50 for myself above my expected expenses. Just as I decide that I'm getting hungry I see something in a gift shop that stops me in my tracks. It's a ceramic picture frame and container set. They have the same pattern: black background, a border that has an Asian flavor and a gold line separating it from the inside pattern that has pink flowers and green leaves. The container has a matching lid and the whole set just fits me. I looked at the price as I held my breath and I was pleased to see they were only $19.95, so I bought them.

Just as I predicted, as soon as the sun started to set the temperature began to drop. I threw on my jacket and ducked into a little restaurant that had the best smell so far wafting from its kitchen. I was already cold, so I ordered a bowl of French onion soup and hot tea. I cradled the tea cup to warm my hands and smelled the fruity aroma as I relaxed and started to look around me. Even though it was autumn, there were still a lot of tourists in the town. As I listened, I could primarily hear French, English, Spanish, and a few languages I didn't recognize. By the posture and expressions, I decided that everyone felt like I did—relaxed. Maybe it's the beautiful environment.

Fortunately, I was fairly close to the motel, so I was only mildly cold when I got back to the room. The tub was surprisingly clean, so I ran the water and poured in some of my bubble bath. I sank down to just relax and try to meditate. It's been a long time since I have even *thought* about Johanna.

But of course, my nervousness about seeing Jennifer tomorrow popped in and that's all she wrote for meditating. I've written to her twice and she is now on the conference calls part of the time, so I know she has softened toward me, but still…

> Dearest Jennifer,
>
> Hi there! How are you holding up? I hope you are doing well and things are getting better. Are you okay now that they took you off of the medication? I thought you might be feeling agitated… that's how it seemed to affect you when you didn't take them here.
>
> I saw the counselor yesterday and we talked about my feelings around all of this. I thought I was just angry, but actually I am sad. I saw that the reason I am sad is that all of your life—from the time you were 2 days old—I had a dream of what life

would be like with us as a family. Things didn't work out that way. Your dad and I couldn't work things out, and then you started down a path that I couldn't walk. Nor could I save you from it.

I realize the dream is not real and that I have to face the reality of what is true: that you are a person who seems very angry and troubled. Your anger seems to be what propelled you through life... as though you wouldn't have survived without it. I'm not sure why you are so angry at your life.

Some of the reasons might be the fact that I moved you 18 times in 17 years and I had no idea we moved that much until I recorded it out of curiosity. I am sorry for that. The fact that three of those times I kept leaving your dad when our attempts at trying to get back together failed... must have been really painful for you. Again, I didn't realize this.

I'm sure the fiasco with David didn't help...you finally got what you wanted all of your life: brothers. And I took you from there too (twice). And the fact that he was abusive didn't help; even though I left as soon as I realized who he was and that no amount of counseling would fix it. I remember that for months after we moved you kept having a nightmare that he murdered me...do you remember?

I apologize for my part in your pain and anger. I did the best I could with the parenting tools I possessed and I know that no parent is perfect, so don't think I'm blaming myself, because I'm not anymore.

I also had to come to the understanding that you are now in charge of your life and, for better or for worse, it's yours to live as you see fit. I wish I could say I'm okay with that. My prayer is that you find yourself and come out of this stronger and better for the experience. My sadness is the knowledge that we may never have the relationship I want for us... that you may never be able to be

*as close to me as I am with Grandma.
It hurts, and it scares me. The sadness
causes me to cry when I think of you
(like now), and my heart isn't the
same without you.*

*I love you so much and I want to
you to know that even though you are
angry with me and feel that I
betrayed you in court, I will never
give up on you or turn you away from
this family. You are an important
part of our lives and our family.*

*I'd better go now, before I flood
the stupid living room with my eyes!*

*I love you, I love you, I love
you…please remember that.*

Mom

I get to the detention compound, which is
outside of town, and enter the office. It takes
quite a while to check me in and to go through
the items I brought. It turns out that visitors
have only two hours a day to see their kids. I am
a little early, so I am invited to join Jennifer's
house at the cafeteria for some lunch.

I wait in the hall so I can give her a hug

when she arrives. The houses start arriving and they walk single file into the building, one house at a time. Finally, I see Jennifer. She waves when she sees me, and she is allowed to get out of line to hug me. Then I join her in line as we enter the cafeteria. We can't speak in line, so we have to wait until we get to the tables. I talk with all the girls at the table and Jennifer seems pleased.

We get back to the house and Jennifer and I go to a corner of the TV room and talk. After an hour or so, we are joined by most of Jenn's housemates, who gather around and we all talk until visiting hours are over.

I get back to the hotel and get on the computer to check my mail and play a game until dinner time. It's after 5:00 when I quit, so I walk next door to the restaurant and order my dinner to go. While I'm waiting, I see a magnificent wall hanging. It's a male and female mallard duck on a piece of wood with the bark still on it. My brother, Dana, collects wooden duck decoys and I think he'll love it. It will take the rest of my spending money, but I decide it's worth it.

The next day I arrive at Jenn's house right on time, and I am welcomed with hugs from all of the girls.

We all sit down and talk. One of the girls sits across from me, leans forward, and smiles genuinely.

I smile back, taken for a moment because she looks and acts so tough. I know from Jenn that she was in a Latino gang. When she walks, there is almost a feral quality to her posture and movements—as though she could pounce whenever it pleases her.

"We all wonder, Mrs. Christy, how such a normal family got stuck wit' a girl like Jenn," she jokes as she points to Jenn with her thumb, jabbing the air at her.

"Just lucky, I guess!" I say as we all burst out laughing.

Then I look at them and say, "Honestly, I wouldn't take back Jennifer for anything—that doesn't mean I loved that last few years—however, I always loved *her*."

"Aww, mom." Jenn grabs me and gives me a quick hug. "I know. I finally know. I think you saved me, mom, really."

Jennifer and I get permission to take a small walk along the perimeter of the houses, which doesn't take long. We sit on a bench outside of her house and talk.

"I guess I shouldn't be surprised that the girls love you," she says.

"What do you mean?"

"Well, a lot of parents never come to see their kids and the ones who do aren't *normal*." She makes air quotes when saying normal.

I raise my eyebrows and look at her sideways. "Normal?"

"Yeah." Her expression changes as she says, "I mean they're drugged up or weird or smell bad…that's why their kids are here, I guess."

"But I am more of a normal picture of a mom for them?"

"Yeah. Hey—I don't mind if they wanna to talk to you and stuff."

"Really? That's *nice*, Jenn." I look at the bushes next to her. "So what do you think happened to *you*, honey…why do you think you ended up here, too?" I look at her gently, accepting.

"Mom, I don't know why but it's like I was determined to do it…all of it. I honestly don't think you could've done anything different—I was determined."

"Thank you for that. I sure wish I knew why, though."

She nods with eyebrows raised as she gazes straight ahead and says in a faraway voice, "Me too."

I say my goodbyes to Jenn outside, then we head back inside, and I say goodbye to the rest of the girls. Many of them hug me and say they hope I come back. I wrap my arm around Jenn's shoulders and say to them as I look at her, "I'm bringing Grandma and Grandpa in May."

"Really mom? Thank you!" She cries as she gives me a rib crushing hug.

When I get home, I start thinking about things with a different perspective. I am more relaxed now that I know it's not a matter of *IF* Jennifer will make it to adulthood, but when. She's getting there, I remind myself.

I think about how long it's been since I spoke to any of my guides. My goodness, I've been so lost for so long! It's not fair that when I really need to speak with them because life has imploded again, the harder it is to reach them. It's a little tough to be open and loving when you're standing in the middle of some strange, alien battle and life once again changes in the blink of an eye. I guess you never know where the day will take you.

I am determined to meditate and see my guides, so I sink into a tub of bubbles and feel my muscles gratefully relax one by one. I deeply breathe in the scent, a sandalwood and rose bubble bath, and quiet my mind. Come on, I urge myself, you can do this. I start breathing in the white light, having to dismiss only a couple of stray thoughts as I clear my energy and fill with the light.

In my mind, I open my eyes and I am in a forest. I can smell the faint vanilla smell of the pines. I see a gigantic cedar tree in front of me…with a door in the trunk. I open the door and step inside. There is another door on the other side. I close the first door and open the new one. When I peer out, I see a sandy beach. I can hear the waves crash into the shore, smell the salt in the air, and feel the warm sun on my face. I step out and close the door absentmindedly. When I turn around, the tree is gone!

"Hello dear one," a voice speaks aloud. It startles me so much that I jump and grab my chest as I turn around.

"Johanna? Is that you? Oh my gosh, you scared me!"

She giggles like a young girl. "Who were you expecting?"

"I didn't really think about it yet. I just got here!"

"Ahhhh," she says with a smile.

Someone else is approaching us now, glimmering with white light. The light shimmers from the heat waves rising from the sand, which makes it look like a mirage. Soon I can see a figure within the light and as he approaches I can see it is Sananda.

"Hello dear one," he says as he reaches us. "We chose this location for our conversation because we know how the ocean is healing and rejuvenating for you."

I nod. It's true that the ocean recharges me.

"Do you have a question for us?" Johanna asks quietly.

"When Jennifer was little, I had these intuitions that she was going to be important in the world—that somehow she was going to make a difference. Now, I just see her struggling to survive."

"There are many times in your history where someone who was troubled or underprivileged as a youth became a leader, a champion, or speaker for what is right."

Sananda adds, "One of your geniuses had learning disabilities and other problems...his name was Albert Einstein. He could not speak well until he was five years old because of his dyslexia. Since that problem was not discovered until much later, his parents thought he was mentally retarded."

We talk for a while longer, and then they bathe me in light and send my awareness back to the tub.

Winter passes quickly and soon it is May. We decide to see Jennifer the first part of the month so dad and I can get back in time to plant the garden. We have set aside a week, so we will have three days with Jennifer. When mom, dad, and I travel, we plan our pit stops around the Indian casinos. Spending time walking around and standing is a nice change from sitting in the car.

When we turn south on Highway 20, we pass through a massive thunderstorm that takes our breaths away. We pull over to enjoy it, since there is no way I want to drive through the downpour. The lightning strikes so often that the thunder sounds continuous.

Then, just as suddenly as it appeared, it is gone and the sun is peeking out. I look east toward the Tetons and there is an amazing double rainbow. After snapping a few photos, we start toward St. Anthony again. We finally arrive at the hotel around 5:30, dead tired and starving.

We head out as soon as visiting time starts so we have plenty of time with Jennifer. When we arrive, Jenn grabs grandma and grandpa excitedly and the other girls come over, too, hugging me and anxious to meet my folks. We stay until visiting time is over, getting hugs from most of the girls as we leave.

The three days pass in a blink and it is already time to go back home.

I decide in June that I need a life again. I find a singles group and meet with them. They are not my type of people, however. Most are overweight and inactive. They mostly meet at restaurants. However, they are having a Fourth of July party and I decide to attend just to get out of the house.

When I get to the backyard party, there are quite a few people there. I gravitate to a couple of ladies that arrive later. We talk and laugh all afternoon. They are both very tan with dark hair. I guess they're in their 50s, although they are both well-built and fit.

I really connect with Darlene and we talk together when we can. Darlene is about 5'4" and in her mid-50s. She laughs easily and seems like a kind person. Her brown-black hair is layered halfway down her back and her bangs frame her face, making it look rounder and… perky. Her eyes are a rich light brown.

After dinner a nice looking man joins us who is around our ages and we all have a great time. Darlene asks if we want to go to the fireworks and we all say yes. We stop by my house to get some camping chairs I have. Everyone piles into my car and we head to the lake. We park several blocks away, lucky to get that close.

Hundreds of people are already on the beach, some having made a day of it. We find a good spot that will fit all of us and we set up. The fireworks over Lake Coeur d'Alene are always magnificent, but this year they were even more spectacular.

Walking back to the car is always a cool and surreal thing. Hundreds of people, waves of humanity, walking in up the blocked-off main streets to their cars. There's a happy, peaceful energy and you know you are totally safe.

When we get back to my house, we exchange phone numbers with promises of keeping in touch. Darlene lingers and we talk a few minutes longer, promising to call one another.

I look for her number several days later and I can't figure out where it has gone. At least she has my number, too. She will probably call me.

However, I don't hear from her. A year passes and I find Darlene's phone number one late July evening in the console of my car. I give her a call and she is so excited. She *just* found my phone number in *her* car and was getting ready to call me. She is currently living in a small town an hour north of me, but in September she is house-sitting in Hayden for the winter. After we hang up, I look up the address and she is only going to be 10 minutes away.

It's October and Jennifer is being released from St. Anthony. She will transition to a group facility in Boise, where she will be taught basic survival skills: working, getting a bank account and keeping it balanced, cooking, finding a place to live, and the like.

Since the winter weather is going to hold off for now, I pack a few of her things and head down to see her right away. It takes a little over nine hours to get to Boise, so it will be a long day.

I get to the hotel fairly late, having stopped for dinner along the way. When I go to see Jennifer the next morning, she has been given a small apartment off of the group facility. It only took her a few hours to find a job at a pizza place, so they rewarded her with the apartment. She will need to start paying rent in November.

The visit goes well and Jennifer is back to the wonderful child I remember…full of promise and glad to be alive. After three days, I have to head back home. I feel confident about Jenn and her progress.

In December, I get a Christmas card with a letter from Jenn. She tells me all about her new life and her new boyfriend. Then I read the last two paragraphs:

> *I did alot of thinking in St. Anthony and I want you to know that I realized so much there. I know you had to send me away. I was so mad at you after court and I was sure you were throwing me away. Just like all my friends parents. But I was wrong. Mom, I just want you to know that I*

get it. I get that you that you did it because you love me and you weren't giving up on me like I thought.

Besides, I think that if you hadn't had me committed then I might not be alive now. I was so close to going way too far.

I start to cry, exclaiming, "She gets it!"

Chapter 19

"You will never know true happiness until you have truly loved, and you will never understand what pain really is until you have lost it." Anonymous

With my daughter's life more or less settled, I concentrate on making a living and taking care of my folks. They don't need me all the time, but when one of them needs me for *anything* I am there. Dad has the most emergencies during the next three years because of arrhythmia. Over the years, his chronic atrial fibrillation has landed him in the ER several times.

One brilliant and beautiful June day, I meet a remarkable man. I had been telling all of my friends that I needed work and I didn't care if it was something other than computer tutoring or writing. One of them mentioned my name to someone who was looking for a housekeeper. I was thrilled! *I* can clean! I call him and we arrange to meet the next day.

I drive to his house to meet him so we can exchange questions. His home is beautiful on the outside. As I approach the door I can see it is highly ornate with a beautifully etched oval glass centerpiece.

When the door opens, the man standing there is exactly my type...*and* he is cute. He is about 5′ 10″ and only slightly heavier than I prefer, but his gorgeous blue eyes and brilliant smile make up for it. His hair is mostly gray and cut short and his reading glasses are perched on top. He is wearing shorts and a short sleeve polo; I can tell he works out.

"Hi, I'm Ben," he smiles as he reaches out to shake my hand, stepping onto the stoop.

I smile at his openness. "Hi. I'm Deborah."

I take his hand and then have to glance away from those eyes, certain I've blushed. I think I might have seen his smile broaden just slightly. He invites me in and closes the door. He takes me on a tour of his home and it is tastefully and expensively decorated. He favors earth tones and deeper blues and greens, whether it is his carpets and tapestry rugs, overstuffed couch and loveseat, his dining room, bathrooms, or most of his window coverings.

I smile at how pleasant his home feels and the warm energy that comes from him. After the tour we sit down to discuss business. We make an agreement and I will start in two days; once a week for now until I get things caught up. Although honestly, from the surface there really isn't much to do so I tell him about two hours a week should work.

He is comfortable with my request to clean while he is at work, so I arrive around 1:00 and get started. I quickly realize there is more to do than I originally thought, but decide it is probable that I am just out of shape. I'm not used to cleaning and scrubbing for two hours straight anymore—not since Jennifer left. There are three of us cleaning our house now, so work is fairly evenly split up. I try to help dad outside as much as I can. Mom still prefers to do most of the upstairs and dad vacuums for her. So once I've cleaned up downstairs and done any work I've got going, I go outside and work in the yard or garden during the summer months and help shovel snow in the winter.

I have to be sneaky about helping dad in the winter. Each year, his stamina decreases, but he refuses to acknowledge it. After all, he is going to be 93 years old this November! So I watch him from the window and when he starts to pant and leans on the shovel, I go out and ask him if I can have a turn…after all, I need the exercise too! He begrudgingly (on the surface) gives me the shovel and says it's just until he catches his breath. Sadly, this happens a little sooner each winter.

Ben starts inviting me over for a glass of wine after the second week and I feel so uncomfortable with it, since I work for him. But one night there's an impending thunder storm and he calls to see if I like watching them because, if I do, his backyard is perfect. Well, I *love* thunder storms so I finally break down and agree to come over.

The lightning and thunder are magnificent. We ooh and aah like a couple of kids, giggling at ourselves and each other. The storm moves to the east and we dart to the left through the first drops of the impending rain to catch more of the lightning. We push ourselves up against the house so the eave protects us from being drenched as the rain moves in sheets, following the storm.

I am so close to Ben that my breath is tickling the back of his neck as he peers out to see when the rain will pass. I see a tiny shudder as he closes his eyes briefly. It doesn't occur to me until I am back home that his actions were a direct result of my breath, which causes an electric shock to shoot through me and I laugh at myself.

We get together several more times and since Ben likes to cook, he makes dinner for us once or twice a week.

About a week after the lightning show I am getting ready to leave and Ben helps me with my sweater near the front door. He stands in front of me with his hands on my shoulders and looks into my eyes. The electric shock shoots through me and my knees feel weak as I look in his blue eyes. He bends down and kisses me very gently, then pulls away a fraction, lingering and breathing me in.

The room gets hot and I feel giddy. As he pulls away and looks into my eyes again, I feel like I am going to explode from the sexual tension. He says goodnight after walking me to my car and gives me another small kiss. When I get home, I pull into the garage and sit there in the quiet. My body has never responded to a man like that in my entire life. Just thinking about it makes me breathless.

I have never been very good at sexual relationships, since my first introductions to it were not healthy. I have loved men, but never really appreciated or truly enjoyed sex with them. So these feelings are new for me. Amazing! This is the first man to really awaken my own sexuality.

The longer we date, the more my body responds to him. I have never reacted to a man like this before, so it is an incredible feeling.

Ben is retired but he does some consulting during the week. He has money, so he takes me to wonderful restaurants and clubs. He has a beautiful boat and he takes me out on lake Coeur d'Alene at least twice a week. We stop at little lakeside cafés and parks for lunch. We take weekend trips when I can get away and my brothers stay with the folks when he takes me to the Caymans for 10 days in December.

Even though we have a great time on our vacation, I can sense something is off between us. Ben tends to withhold love when he is upset with me, which boggles my mind. Sometimes he won't even say why he is angry, and trying to talk with him and explain that withholding love is not okay with me does no good whatsoever.

But there is more to it than that. I finally find a guy that I want to be with sexually (and can't seem to get enough of), and he doesn't seem to be sexually aroused by me. Not when I give him a full body massage, not when I dance seductively for him, not when I walk around naked. I have to ask to be intimate or he doesn't seem to think of it.

As the weeks pass it becomes more and more obvious that Ben is not attracted to me…I'm not sure he finds me attractive at all anymore.

Ben talks about getting a dog a few times. While he is in Arizona visiting his kids, I get a strong feeling to go to the local shelter. I walk through the kennel looking at all the dogs as they bark and jump and try to get my attention. I get to a large kennel that has a curtain behind it and there is a border collie. She looks so sad. Her ears are down and her big brown doe eyes are watching me. I reach in and touch her, then look to see the card that tells you about that particular dog, but there isn't one. Suddenly, a woman comes flying out from behind the curtain and grabs the dog.

"How did you get out of your cage? Your supposed to be in quarantine!" She exclaims as she takes the dog behind the curtain.

I walk to the office and ask if there is some way to let them know I am interested in her. There is a waiting list, I am told, so I have her put my name on down. I am the first on the list.

Ben gets home two days later and I take him to see the dog. We get to the same kennel and she is there. Ben talks to her and reaches in to touch her as I notice she is shaved nearly to her skin. I shake my head. Why would anyone shave a dog in January — especially since this is one of the coldest, snowiest winters ever?

Suddenly, the same woman comes flying out from behind the curtain again, repeating her confusion about how the dog gets out.

"This is the second time you have escaped!" She says, breathlessly.

Ben is not willing to commit to a pet right now, so we leave. I go back the next day and she is out of quarantine, so I take her for a walk in their enclosed field. There is too much snow for a decent walk, so I find a steel bench in an enclosure that's about 12 feet square. The bench is dry, since it is beneath a huge Douglas fir.

There is a tennis ball and I throw it for her once I get the leash off, but she doesn't even look at it. She just sits up against my leg and looks at me with those huge brown eyes; then she lifts her paw and places it on my knee.

"Awwwwwww, you are so cute!"

I walk her back inside and we go up to the office so I can ask about the waiting list. I am seriously thinking about taking her home.

"I'm sorry, but your name is not on the list for her."

"What do you mean? I put my name in on Monday."

"Someone put your name on a list the day after we received her?"

I nod.

"I am so sorry, but we are not allowed to start a waiting list until the animal has been here for five days. We want to give their owners time to find them; plus we quarantine them during that time. There is only one name on the list. Would you like me to add yours to it?"

"Yes, please."

I walk out, thinking: if it is meant to be, she will be mine. I talk to the folks about it that night during dinner. I know that mom will probably be against it. She never fully recovered from the death of her little dog, Heidi.

Surprisingly, once I tell them about the dog,

mom says it's okay with her. Dad, however, also surprised me.

"I'm not in favor of it," he says.

"Why not, dad?"

"I can't bear to outlive another pet."

"Well she is only 2 years old dad and you are 94. Are you planning to be around in 15 years?" I say with a slight smile.

He sits up straight and looks at me. All he says is, "Maybe!"

We laugh and talk some more and mom has convinced him to let me bring her home. I explain that it might not even be an issue, since my name is second on the list.

I go back the next day and walk her again. I want to get to know her better. It's hard, though, since she has no interest in playing. She just looks me in the eyes with her paw on my knee. When we get back, one of the ladies starts up a conversation about her and how gentle she seems to be. We talk a few more minutes while I pet the dog's head and then I take her back to her kennel.

I get a call Saturday morning from the same lady. She says that the dog is now eligible for adoption. The man with his name at the top of the list is still interested.

"I am calling you first because the dog doesn't look at him the way she looks at you. If you still want her, I will tell him that the owners picked her up. This is not how we do things, so you can't say anything to the other employees about it, okay?"

"No problem!" I exclaim. "When can I pick her up?"

"You have to get her today."

I run to the store and pick up bowls and food and a collar and leash. Then I go pick her up. She seems confused, but gets into the car with me. The first thing I do is give her a bath to get the kennel smell off of her. We decide that a good Scottish dog like a border collie needs a good Scottish name, so we agree on Molly.

I take her to Ben's that night so he can meet her and he falls in love with her. I realize that I'm glad he didn't want her. They play and snuggle on the carpet while I watch, smiling.

I've had her about a week now and she seems to be settling in nicely. Dad avoids touching her. He doesn't want to fall in love with her. Of course, that doesn't last long!

One day I have her outside so I can vacuum and she wants in. She eventually heads off the porch and back into the yard. I finish and turn off the vacuum so I can put it away. That's when I heard it.

There was a strange banging noise and I can hear a dog wailing and howling. I go out back to see if it's Molly and I find her on the side of the house. The neighbor is working in his yard and Molly is hanging by her front legs on the six foot wooden gate, crying and trying to see the neighbor.

I call her and she jumps down and comes to me, uncertain. I squat down so I am closer to her and give her a hug.

"It's okay, honey. You're safe now." She follows me into the house and never tries to escape again.

Mom and dad want to know what happened. I tell them the story of what I saw and finish by saying, "It was as though she was trying to get Steve's attention. It looked like she was saying, help! I'm trapped and I can't get out!"

It turns out that border collies are really intelligent and Molly is no exception. She is fairly easy to train and she minds very well.

Ben and I have a Super Bowl party and invite all of our friends. Everyone is taking pictures with their phones, including me. I am given a photo from one of our friends the last week in May, after complaining to her about the way Ben is acting toward me. It's a picture of Ben talking to another friend, Mary. I look carefully at his face and body language. I sigh sharply as the pain stabs through me, practically doubling me over. It's obvious now why he is cool toward me. I have decided that I have to leave him, but it is so painful that I keep putting it off.

I knew Mary for about a year before I met Ben. She was a friend and office neighbor of the counselor I was seeing during the Jennifer phase. She was always kind to me and we got along well. I even helped her kids' fundraisings by buying whatever they were selling. I had no idea she knew Ben until we started dating. She seemed so happy for us.

Mary is only about 5'2" with a slight build, auburn hair, and a pale (almost gray), complexion. I attributed her coloring to the fact that she chain smoked. She is over twenty years younger than Ben. Some of his comments about the rich guys and their trophy wives make a little more sense now.

We go out on the boat two weeks later and my mind is occupied with thoughts of leaving and salvaging what's left of my heart. We stop at the gas dock to fill up and I jump out to tie off the boat as usual. I forget that I have taken off my sneakers and put on my aqua shoes. As I grab the rope and jump onto the deck, my feet slip and swivel and I am flipped up against the boat while still holding the rope so my arm is smashed behind me.

The pain is so bad in my shoulder that I am in shock and all I can do is sit on the dock, rocking. When Ben realizes something is wrong, he jumps out, ties off the boat, then checks on me. By the time he gets the boat back into its slip and helps me to the truck, the shock starts to wear off and the pain has me in tears. It turns out that I fractured the humerus in two places.

Ben brings me home and we sit down on the couch downstairs. I ask him to explain how he sees our relationship.

He looks down at his hands and says, "Best friends?"

"Best friends...I guess that makes sense."

The pain medication is making me sleepy, so I decide it's a good excuse to have Ben leave. To make matters worse, Mary comes over the next day to bring me some aromatherapy oils. She doesn't know that I know about them. I thank her for the oils and watch her face as I tell her I think Ben and I are breaking up. I fight back tears as she says how sorry she is, but I can see it in her eyes—what is it, relief?

The rest of the year is hard to live through and seems to be passing interminably slow. The pain of losing the man I thought could possibly be my soulmate is overwhelming most of the time. Now I know how Al felt…he thought I was *his* soulmate but I was unable to return that depth of love.

After Ben and I broke up and he was dating Mary within a month. In the fall, Mary decides (for reasons I can't begin to understand) to bad mouth me around town. She accuses me of doing most the things that Ben did to me: emotionally withdrawn, unloving, lying, and so on. She even made up a story about how I tried to tell Ben how to handle his remodel and made demands of the contractor! The strangest part is that those things are completely unlike me and she has to know that.

All the drama settles down after I talk with Ben about the hurtful things she is saying—apparently he talked to her about it.

They end up getting married in November. He gets his trophy wife.

Dad is hospitalized twice this fall for his arrhythmia and in late December he develops congestive heart failure. He has a myriad of tests done and in January the heart doctor tells him to settle his affairs. His heart muscles have hardened from all of the years of arrhythmia and he is in danger of going into renal failure. Dad is 94 but he looks well over 10 years younger. Today, as we get home from the doctor, he looks his age.

The doctor suggests we get started with hospice so they can help as his needs increase. This will take some of the burden off of me, since we also just found out last week that mom needs a hip replacement. She is planning to have it done in February.

Dad is having trouble with his balance and stamina, so hospice provides him with a nice walker with a seat. They also bring him a wheelchair for going out to appointments.

We find a great geriatric doctor who comes to the house for appointments, so mom and dad both get signed up. What a relief! That will save me from spending the day at doctors' offices.

Mom goes in for her surgery and despite dad's own problems, he looks so scared for her. Everything goes well, however, and she is in an assisted living facility called Life Care for rehab about a week later. I make dinner most nights and dad and I take it to Life Care and have dinner with mom.

Dad carries the food on his lap and I wheel him in. They allow pets, so I bring Molly with us. The residents love her so I take her down the halls when we come to visit so she can make the rounds. She is so well-behaved that I don't even put her on a leash.

One night, dad wakes up from his evening nap around 8:30 and calls to me. He sounds panicky, so I rush in. He is sitting on the edge of the bed as I approach him, looking down.

"I thought I was perspiring, but my pant leg is all wet—too wet for sweat."

I reach down and feel his left pants leg and it is soaking wet. He changes into his pajamas and I have him go out to the living room and sit in the recliner so I can get a better look. His calves are really swollen, but the left one is biggest and a pink fluid is pooling and leaking from several places on his lower leg. I can't see any tears or cuts when I wipe away the fluid, so I am at a loss.

I jump on the computer and look up what's happening. I find articles that explain it: he has weeping edema. I have never heard of this before, but I read up on what to do.

Apparently, when edema causes his leg to swell, the skin is stretched to its limit. If there is any weak spot on the skin, the fluid will leak out there. It is pink because of red blood cells. I grab a chair from the kitchen and rest his leg on a folded towel. I wrap his leg in gauze bandages, and leave his pant leg up so it doesn't get wet. Within an hour, the gauze is getting wet and the edema is still weeping.

I call hospice and talk with the on-call attendant. Even though it is nearly 11:00, he says he will stop by the office for supplies and be over within an hour. John arrives at almost 12:30

and I feel so badly that he is out her so late, but I am also incredibly grateful. He brought all kinds of absorbent pads, gauze, tape, gloves, and ointments.

He compliments how I wrapped dad's leg and then shows me how to use the pads and gauze he brought. He explains about edema and tells me to call his doctor tomorrow.

I call the doctor's office and they are sending out the doctor today. Dr. Jains arrives around 2:00 and looks over dad's legs. As I put new pads on his leaks, the doctor is going over what looks like lab results. Dad lies down for a nap when Dr. Jains finishes with him.

She chats with me as she packs up her laptop and medical gear, approving of my care of dad and explaining a few more things. She had asked for dad's heart doctor's notes and went over them in detail, explaining things I couldn't understand.

I walk her to the door and as she puts on her boots and coat, she lowers her voice.

"I'm really sorry to do this to you, but you have to make a decision. Your dad is terminal no matter what we do at this point. The only difference is quality of life for his remaining time. Here is your choice: we can give him a diuretic for his congestive heart failure, which will reduce the fluid in his lungs. It will also help with his edema. If we give him the diuretic, however, we will hasten renal failure from his weakened kidneys.

"I know that it sounds like there is only one choice, but let me explain a little about renal failure. First of all, the kidneys will not be able to filter waste from the blood as well. It could make it more difficult to urinate — diuretics increase urination."

"If we treat the congestive heart failure, will he breathe more easily?"

"Definitely. The fluid will be gone."

"Then that's what I choose. Dad expressed a real fear of struggling for breath. I think he would rather breathe comfortably. Are there options to help the renal failure symptoms?"

"Yes and we will talk about those in about a week. I want to check the lab results for the blood I've drawn today and research a little more. Hospice will bring George's medications tomorrow at the latest."

I am struggling about whether to tell him or not…do I have the right to make that decision? What about mom? Do I ask her? Is she even in a position to help me choose? I'm not sure *I* could be after living with him for over 62 years.

I call each of my brothers and ask their opinions. They feel I am making the best decision for dad but they don't know what to do about telling him, either. They each defer to my judgment, since I will be responsible for both dad *and* mom. After letting me know they are there for me if I need anything, I say goodbye to each conversation and promise regular updates. I really love my family.

When we get home from having dinner with mom, dad goes to lie down. While he is napping I make the decision to talk with him about his health.

I tell him everything while he sips on a little coffee and wakes up. At the end, he looks at me with compassion and love.

"I'm sorry you were put in that position and I appreciate how hard making that choice was for you. You were right, though… I would rather be able to breathe."

Mom comes home two weeks later and we have home health nursing assistance for her, which helps a great deal. She is using a walker and I get the feeling she will be using it from now on, since her back still hurts her.

While I was with Ben, I had a tough time finding and keeping work. The recession was in full swing and the freelance writing sites were bombarded with people in the Philippines and

Puerto Rico who were willing to work for $3.00 an hour!

Ben paid for me to have a month's worth of business coaching. The coaching was great and I loved my coach, but it wasn't much help. I didn't know what to do for work or where to concentrate my efforts. What I did realize, however, was that writing and freelance tech support no longer paid the bills. They were a luxury people could do without.

➡

Chapter 20

"Repeat to yourself the most comforting words of all: This, too, shall pass." Ann Landers

It's a beautiful and warm March evening, so I take Molly for a ride and run to the market. I do my shopping and we head back home. While I am waiting to cross Highway 95, I turn and talk to Molly in the back seat and pet her.

The light changes and we head across the four lane highway. Just as we are nearly out of the intersection, we start moving sideways. I look down at the speedometer for some reason just as the car lifts off the ground and starts to flip. Then it slams down on the driver's side, bouncing twice and sliding what seems like forever down Kathleen Street.

I am completely confused. I can't figure out what just happened. I guess a car hit me, but I didn't see it. WAIT! Where's Molly? I have been so stunned by everything that I forgot to look for her. I struggle to turn my head and look in the back. I can see her. She looks okay. She is in the very back of the 4-Runner, standing on a shattered window.

"Are you okay, Molly?"

She just looks at me totally confused. Poor

thing! I've only had her a little over a month! People are running up to the car to check on me. One guy keeps asking me to show him my left arm. He was in the car behind me and saw my arm out the window while we were waiting to cross the highway.

My arm is fine and I show him just as the Fire Department shows up. I ask one of the firemen to call my neighbor to see if he will come and get Molly. The car is smashed on the passenger side, so they pop out the sun roof and help me crawl out.

When I look back I see Molly being handed out of the car, and I feel so badly for her. Steve has arrived and he takes Molly into his car as two firemen help me to the ambulance. My knees give out and they grab onto me.

Stupidly, I say, "Drunk again!" Then I look at them with wide eyes and say, "I'm joking, guys. I don't drink."

One of them nods and says that there is no alcohol smell on me so not to worry. Whew! A policeman speaks to me while the paramedics are checking me out.

Apparently, a teenage girl with a new license was driving with her friends and was so engrossed that she never saw the red light. She only had a few feet to respond. That's why I didn't hear tires screeching. She was driving a small Toyota sedan.

I ask if the kids are okay and he says, "Surprisingly, no one was seriously injured."

After checking me out thoroughly, the ER releases me. Steve is waiting to take me home. He and his wife are mom's age and they are the most wonderful neighbors. I thank him profusely when we get home.

I check on Molly. She seems in shock, but otherwise okay. I take her to the vet in dad's car when I am well enough to drive. Dr. Anderson is the best vet I have ever met. When I tell her about the accident, she gets down on the floor next to Molly to check her out. She literally checks every vertebrae and then pokes and prods the rest of her. Nothing broken or seriously damaged.

A couple of weeks later, I am surfing the web looking for work when I find an ad for Certified Life Coaching certification. I remember my business coach and I think to myself, *that's it*! That's what I want to do! When I was in college after high school, I was intending to go into counseling to help kids like me.

I choose a certification program and sign up for the online courses. My wonderful State Farm agent gets me the money for my car quickly, knowing I will need to find another one soon. I use some of it to pay for my certification course.

Spring passes too quickly into summer, it seems. Molly and I take dad for a walk in his wheelchair whenever it's at least 80°. We walk along the greenbelt and dad walks a few steps for exercise while I keep the wheelchair close behind him.

Summer seems to fly, since I am now trying to keep up with dad's yard work, help mom with the housework, cook, shop, care for them, and work at my business. I have several clients now.

It's the end of October and dad is deteriorating more each day. He and mom celebrate their 63rd wedding anniversary on the 26th, which is dad's goal. He wants to make it to their anniversary. On the 29th, he wakes up in the morning and I can tell this is it. I call Hospice and they come take care of him with meds and soft words. When they have done all they can, they give me instructions and leave. Mom and I take turns sitting with him and the fear on his face causes me to start talking of it. I tell him how I believe, that we are more than our bodies. After all, he believes we are energy like I do. I tell him my belief that once we are free of our bodies that we become part of everything. It's not the end, just a transition to another reality.

It's four o'clock and I head down to the office with a married couple I am coaching and mom sits with dad. When we come upstairs, mom is standing in the doorway to the bedroom looking down. My heart flip-flops as I realize that dad may be gone. I walk my clients to the door and say goodbye. I turn to mom.

"Five minutes ago, but I'm not sure. Will you check him?" mom says as I walk over to her.

She follows me in the bedroom and dad is still. His mouth is wide open like he was taking a deep breath. I take his chin and gently try to close his mouth but it resists. I listen for his heart and check his pulse. Nothing. I try to close his mouth again now I know I can't hurt him, but it still won't budge.

"Leave it," mom says.

I call the funeral home and they come and get him. They close his mouth before bringing him out. We say our goodbyes when they pause for us.

Naturally, Mom is not dealing well. She cries much of the time and talks very little. Things improve as time goes by and she seems more at peace with everything, but of course she can't talk about him yet without crying.

Dad's birthday was in November, so the holidays are really hard for mom. I don't seem to be grieving. I haven't felt like crying and I am not torn up like mom has been. I wonder if I'm in denial, but I don't think so. I think I had enough time to come to terms with it. Besides, the quality time I have had with him all this year has been so wonderful. I think that perhaps I don't feel like grieving because I have no regrets. I said all the things I wanted to say and loved him unconditionally.

Life has settled down a little bit. It's the second week in April and I am showing mom plans for this summer's vegetable garden.

"Are you all right, mom?" I ask her. She looks uncomfortable, like she's in pain.

"I'm okay. I just feel a heaviness in my chest. I think it's heartburn. I'll take an antacid."

"Okay." I look at her face as I turn to leave. It seems like more than heartburn.

Over the next few days, Mom looks and does fine all day but gets that weird pain in her chest every night—particularly when she lays down to sleep. On the fourth night I start asking her to go to the hospital or at least call her doctor. She refuses the hospital and promises to call the doctor if she still feels badly the next morning; but of course, she's always better in the morning.

It's been six days and when I bring her morning juice, she looks gray.

"Mom, I'm sorry but I'm not taking no for an answer. You look terrible. I want to take you to the hospital."

"I think so, too. I don't feel right."

Oh God! My heart sank to my toes and then jumped into my throat. "Can you get up and dress or would you like help?"

"I'll just put on my robe and we can go."

Mom *never* leaves the house undressed. "Okay. Stay here. I will start the car and get everything ready. I'll be right back."

I flew out the door and got everything ready in minutes, including letting Molly out and feeding her. She's able to use the walker and get to the car. I load her up and put her walker in the back. She doesn't talk much, just sits there looking straight ahead.

I pull into the hospital and the valets open the doors. "I need a wheelchair for my mom, please."

The valet takes one look at my mom and runs into the doorway and grabs a wheelchair. I wheel her in and tell the receptionist that I think mom's heart may be in trouble. She makes a call and before I can give her mom's name, a nurse appears and takes us into triage. She takes mom's blood pressure and gets some details from us, then she gets up abruptly and rushes out the door. She returns seconds later with another nurse who grabs mom and takes us down the hallway to the rooms. There is a flurry of activity in a room directly in front of us and we enter into the fray. They part for mom and I step into the doorway to stay out of the way.

They have her undressed and in the bed in record time, hooking her up to machines and starting IVs simultaneously. All of the ER visits with dad's heart problems didn't prepare me for this. I knew we were in trouble by the speed and concentrated effort being spent on her.

A tall, thin male nurse asks, "Does she have a heart doctor?"

I tell him no, but I like dad's heart doctor, Dr. Spire. He nods and leaves. They are admitting her right away, so the activity continues all around us for quite a while. They've finally allowed me to sit next to her, so I pull up a chair and we hold hands.

We talk a little, but the heart monitor's alarm keeps going off and distracts me. I've seen a lot of monitors with vital signs because of dad, and his would go off all the time too—he was throwing PVCs. But mom's is very different. It's going wild with BP alarms, heart rate alarms, and more.

Surprisingly, Dr. Spire arrives within 30 minutes. He listens to our story of how she has been over the last week and then checks all the test results.

"You are having a heart attack, Mrs. Carr," he starts. "In fact, you have been having a low-grade heart attack for a week."

"Is that possible?" I ask.

"Oh yes. Unfortunately, it has damaged the heart. We need to take her into surgery right away."

"But I don't want you to open my chest," mom says, barely above a whisper."

"We will enter through an artery in your groin and work up to your heart to see what's going on. We will decide what to do from there. We may be able to clean out the arteries to open them up."

Mom is wheeled into surgery within 30 minutes. While she is in the operating room I call Dana and tell him what is happening. He decides to drive up to be with me. He should be here in about six hours. Then I call my best friend, Darlene. She is coming over to stay at the house to take care of Molly while I am at the hospital.

Three hours later, the doctors come out. Dr. Spire looks at me compassionately. "Your mother's arteries are 80% occluded. Honestly, it's a miracle she's still alive."

"What can you do?"

"We are going to have to put in a stent to open up the atrial artery. That will increase blood flow substantially. Her ventricle heart valve is damaged, which is also dangerous for her."

"I have asked a specialist to come in and perform the surgery. It will be several hours before he arrives, so we are taking her to her room for now and keeping a close eye on her."

I stay with mom in her room in the cardiac ward and we visit a little bit. Mostly, she drifts in and out because she is sedated to keep her calm.

Dana arrives around 8:00 and stays with her while I get something to eat. An hour later the doctors are ready to operate. They wheel her to the operating rooms and stop in front of the entrance to speak with Dana and me. There are four doctors explaining everything and answering questions, which in itself is unnerving. I've never seen that many surgeons taking that much time with anyone before.

One of the doctors looks at us and says, "All of her veins and arteries are 80% occluded with plaque. We will try to clean out her major arteries and insert the stent. There are many reasons this may not work. We could possibly lose her on the table to a heart attack. The plaque can break loose and lodge in her heart or brain. This will be very risky."

"But there is no other option, is that correct?" Dana asks.

"No. Without it she will die."

We nod and look at each other.

Then mom touches Dr. Spire's hand, which is on the bed rail, and begs them not to crack her chest.

"We won't need to. We will enter through the artery in your groin and work up to your heart to insert the stent."

She nods and drops her hand, closing her eyes with a big sigh. Dana and I kiss her and tell her we love her and they take her in.

Time seems to drag as we wait. Three and a half hours later, Dr. Spire enters the waiting room. His face is serious and tired.

"We were able to get the stent in and clean out the most important arteries, but plaque broke away and went to her heart. She had a heart attack on the table and we nearly lost her several times. We also verified that her left ventricular valve is not working properly, which will need to be addressed down the line.

"We have her on a tandem heart, which will help her heart beat until she is more stable. We inserted it through the groin on her right side. We have inserted an intra-aortic balloon pump to increase blood flow while her heart is weak. We will have to keep her in a medicated coma until the tandem heart and balloon pump are removed so she doesn't move. We hope to have them out in 48 hours. She will also remain on the ventilator."

Dana and I get to the house around 1:00 in the morning. I get him set up in the second guest room, peek in on Darlene, let Molly out to go potty, and then collapse into bed.

Dana takes me out to breakfast the next morning and then we head over to the hospital. Mom has stabilized and they are planning to remove the balloon pump today, so Dana heads home to go back to work.

They also remove the tandem heart when they remove the balloon pump. If her heart holds its own, then the breathing tube can come out in two days. I spend the day with mom every day, even though she doesn't know I'm here. I go home a couple of times to see Darlene and Molly and grab food, since I am only 10 minutes from the hospital.

It's been two days and mom is still not responding to requests to open her eyes, so the ventilator stays in overnight again. They have cut down on the pain meds to encourage her to wake up, but I worry she is in pain. She grimaces a lot now that her meds are cut in half. I feel so helpless—all I can do is sit here and watch her struggle.

This morning I attended Grand Rounds. This is where the nurses, doctors, and family discuss the patient at length to get everyone's insights. Mom has developed pneumonia over night and she still can't squeeze our hands or open her eyes for more than a second.

When Dr. Spire comes in, he takes me outside the room to speak with me. His face is serious and concerned.

"As you know, when we cleaned out the artery last week some of the plaque broke away on the operating table. Now we are concerned that a piece may have gone toward her brain stem and caused neurological damage, which means she won't improve. Our concern is that the reason she is not waking up is because the plaque could have caused her to have a stroke. We will do a CAT scan later today.

When they take her for the CAT scan, I head to the cafeteria to grab a quick bite. When I return to the room, mom is just getting back and the nurses are getting her hooked up again. The doctor returns for his evening rounds a few hours later and tells me that the scan was clear and that she has not had a stroke.

We step outside the room and he looks at me for a few moments and then says, "During your mother's heart attacks on the table, her brain was deprived of oxygen several times. There is a possibility that she has suffered some brain damage."

When he sees the look on my face, Dr. Spire puts his hand on my shoulder and looks at me compassionately. Between mom and dad, he knows what I have been through.

They decide not to push her to wake up until the pneumonia clears. They want to give her a day or two.

Mom is a little more awake this morning, but still out of it. I am worried about the blood thinners...she's bleeding under the skin of her arms and legs and she looks a little like a boxer after a bout!

Mom and I both took in foster kids — she had all ages of kids, including teenagers and I specialized in babies and toddlers. Most of the older kids have kept in touch with her, and in some cases, they consider her like their mom. One of the younger girls who stayed with mom on and off for years, calls her Grandma and even took the last name Carr when she became a citizen. I like to introduce Deyna as my sister, especially if mom is with us...then we really confuse people when she calls mom Grandma!

One of mom's foster boys, Randy, has

become a son to her and a brother to me. He's in his 40s now and when he heard about mom, he flew up from Texas to see her and to help me with whatever I need. Melissa and their daughter Zoe could not join him this time.

It is hard for him to see her like this. She's got tubes coming out from everywhere and her skin is all blotched black and blue and red from the blood thinners she is on. The ventilator is an imposing piece of technology, particularly when it is inserted in someone you love. Her skin is still an ash gray from all the trauma.

When he is not at the hospital, Randy is helping with chores around the house. This gives Darlene a break from caring for the house and Molly.

Mom still cannot pass the breathing test but she did better than ever before, so I am hopeful. She squeezed the nurse's hands for the first time and can respond to a question or two by nodding or shaking her head.

She is responding to questions now. She can shrug her shoulders and nod and shake her head. She can open her eyes more, but still can't keep them open yet. She is able to stay awake longer now, too.

She is grimacing more than usual tonight and Randy and I are trying to figure out what she needs.

"Are you hurting, mom?" I ask her.

She nods.

"Is it the breathing tube?"

She shakes her head. I name a few more locations, but get nowhere.

"Let's try the alphabet." Randy suggests.

"Okay. Let us know when we get to the first letter of your body part, okay?"

She nods.

"A, B, C..." I get to the end of the alphabet but she doesn't nod at any of the letters. I look at Randy and he shakes his head.

"Did I go too fast, mom?"

She nods.

"Oh! Okay, here we go. A..."

She nods quickly.

"It starts with A?" Randy clarifies.

She nods.

Randy and I look at each other. His eyes light up and he smiles.

"Mom, is it your ass?" he asks.

She nods emphatically.

We break out laughing and mom tries to laugh with us. I go get the nurse and she and I help her change positions.

Randy can only stay four days, but it has

been so nice to see him. After we say our goodbyes I head back to the hospital.

Today is the first time I have felt like it's going to be okay. I notice that she can't move her right foot yet but she is moving her left foot nicely. She can squeeze with both hands now, too. We will have to wait until she is breathing on her own and talking before we will know how she is doing neurologically.

I sit next to her and watch Netflix on my iPhone while she sleeps, helping her as needed and getting the nurse when her breathing tube needs clearing or she needs pain management. I head home around 5:30 and have dinner with Darlene, who has returned to help out.

I get to the hospital this morning in time for Grand Rounds. The nurse is saying that her right foot is finally moving. She is passing the breathing test today, but they still don't want to extubate her for another day or two. She looks worn out this morning, so I can't really tell if she is better or not. They are planning to keep mom asleep tomorrow so they can exercise her lungs in preparation for removing the ventilator, so I am spending the day at home with Molly and Dar.

I spend the morning leisurely, which feels wonderful. The three of us go for a walk in the afternoon. Even though it's only about 50 degrees, it feels so good to be outside. The sun is out and I lift my face to enjoy it.

When I get to the hospital this morning, they are concerned with her numbers, which have to do with her oxygen levels and other things. They have decided not to remove the ventilator, again, worried she will not be able to breathe on her own.

It is very undesirable to remove and then reinsert the tube, because it can permanently damage her vocal cords. This is also their concern for leaving the tube in as long as they have...not to mention the danger of stenosis, which is the narrowing of the trachea.

There is always a sense of trade-offs and gambling in every turn with mom. It can be maddening for the loved ones who are watching and waiting.

Another concern the doctor's have mentioned is the extra load on her heart once she is breathing on her own. They wonder if her heart can take it. However, the risks to her trachea and lungs are so high that during his evening rounds, the doctor has decided to remove the tracheal tube in the morning. Twelve days on a ventilator is a very long time.

I head home, worrying about everything. I am thrilled she is coming off the ventilator, but terrified her heart won't be able to handle it. It's hard to know what to think and sleep is eluding me tonight.

I arrive back at the hospital around 8:30, since the doctors want to take the tube out after grand rounds. I sit with mom and we hold hands while we wait. She is more awake this morning...it's probably the anticipation keeping her more alert. The nurses come in around 9:30 and ask me to stand in front of the bed.

"Seeing a trusted face helps with the panic when we remove the tube," one of the nurses says.

"Why would she panic?"

"When the tube is coming out, there is a feeling of gagging that can scare the patient."

"Okay."

I stand in front of the bed and the nurse raises the head of the bed, which sits mom straight up. They pull down her covers and remove the leg pumps from around her ankles. These pumps remind me of blood pressure sleeves. They fill and release air to keep patients from developing blood clots.

"Okay Esther, I want you to cough for me when I tell you to."

Mom nods. One of the nurses releases the balloon that keeps the tube from coming out of her throat.

"Okay Esther, COUGH! Cough for me, keep coughing." She is pulling the tube as she talks to mom. When the tube finally slips out, mom's head drops to her chest.

She looks so small now in that bed. It's very strange. They lift her head and set the bed back just enough to keep her head upright. They work around her for a while, making sure she is breathing well enough on her own. When they are satisfied, they set her head back a little more so she can rest. Just removing the tube has exhausted her. She grimaces that her throat hurts, but the nurse tells her that she can't give her anything until she passes the swallowing test.

"The speech-language pathologist will be her in an hour to give you a swallowing assessment to test your swallowing ability. From there we will know what we can give you, okay Esther?"

Mom nods, but doesn't look happy. I take her hand and smile at her and she smiles back. Finally! I can see her face, lips, and teeth and she can finally close her mouth.

"Isn't there anything we can do for her?" I ask.

"Here, you can use some of the swabs we used to keep her mouth from drying out while on the ventilator. Don't let her suck on it yet, though—not until the therapist gives the okay.

The risk of the liquid going into her lungs is too great."

"Why is that?"

"When the tube is kept in as long as your mom's, there is the danger of aspiration. This is when liquid or solids are not swallowed right and they enter the lungs instead. This increases the possibility of pneumonia or infection."

"Okay."

I am used to the swabs, since I helped keep her mouth moistened with them over the last week. I open one and swab her mouth, tongue, and teeth. Mom closes her eyes in relief as I take another and keep swabbing.

Dr. Spire comes in early today, smiles and gives my shoulder a squeeze. He walks up to mom and starts talking to her.

"Hello Esther, do you know who I am?"

Mom nods and whispers, "You're Dr. William Spire from the North Idaho Heart Institute."

He looks at her surprised and she giggles. She points to his jacket and says, "I read your smock."

He laughs with her and then asks her more questions. He checks her out and then gives me a bright smile and says, "I think her brain is just fine."

I reach for my chest and smile back with a

huge sigh of relief. "Thank you," is all I can manage to say.

After he leaves a woman enters the room and introduces herself as Julie, the speech-language pathologist. She has a cart with several items on it.

"The first thing we normally do is a water test, where we give the patient about three ounces of water to drink. But because of the length of time your mom has been intubated, we already know she will have difficulty swallowing thin liquids. I am going to start with a thick, lemon-flavored nutritional supplement.

"Esther," she starts as she raises the head of mom's bed, "I have something for you to try and eat. I need you to concentrate on swallowing so it stays out of your lungs."

Mom points to her throat and shakes her head.

"It's okay, Esther, this is like a frozen lemonade and it will feel good on your throat. Will you try?"

Mom nods yes and takes a tiny amount into her mouth. She swallows carefully, wincing slightly. Her eyes have been mostly closed but once she swallows her eyes pop open wide and she makes an mmmmmm sound, letting us know it tastes good.

She gets two more small spoonfuls and

opens her mouth for more, but Julie shakes her head.

"That's all for right now, Esther. We have to go slowly. I've asked the nurses to order a throat spray for you to help with the irritation. I will be back every two hours to test your swallowing."

Mom is clearly disappointed but nods that she understands. I, however, feel elated. I can see now that she is going to mend.

Julie returns as promised three more times. On the last visit, she tries a couple of spoonfuls of peach yogurt. All seems to be going well, although mom's throat is really sore. We finally get the throat spray that evening and it seems to help.

The doctor comes in for his evening visit and says that he is not happy with her oxygenation tests and he wants to put her on a BiPAP machine. I have heard of a CPAP but not BiPAP. I ask him the difference and he explains that the BiPAP helps control the incoming air like the CPAP, but also helps with the exhale as well.

His hope is that it will not only help her breathe, but also help exercise her lungs to strengthen them. He only expects her to stay on it for around 24 hours.

The nurses come in with the machine and place the mask over her mouth and nose. It is very loud and at first mom looks a little panicky that it is forcing her to take breaths but soon relaxes and looks comfortable, so I take off for the night.

Wednesday

Today is a little better for mom. She came off the BiPAP around 1:00 and Julie will be coming in for more swallowing tests. Mom's voice is a hoarse whisper and she is easily confused, but I can hear her requests and see her smile, which makes me happy. She is very weak, so I help her as much as I can.

They start giving her blood this afternoon, because she is losing it from somewhere. They suspect it's leaking from her bowel, so they cut down on the blood thinners. She's not well enough for the rehab facility, so the doctor wants to move her to a long-term specialty hospital until she is ready for rehab.

I head home a little early this evening to spend time with Darlene and watch a movie together. We start the movie at 7:00 and at 7:45 I get a call from the hospital. It's mom! I can barely hear her hoarse whisper, but she tells me that the nurses are holding her down and won't let her get into bed.

I am so confused! She couldn't have gotten out of bed when I was there, so it makes no sense. I get dressed and head back to the hospital to check on her and find out what's going on. The door I normally enter is locked for the night, so I head across the grass to the main doors. As I am walking up a small rise, I slip and literally flip up into the air and land on my arm, bending my wrist back. It hurts so much, but all I can think of is getting to mom.

I finally get to her room and she is sitting in a recliner while the nurses are cleaning her bed and removing equipment she no longer needs. I talk to the nurse and she said that mom got very upset when they took her out of the bed and insisted on calling me. They dialed for her and then went back to cleaning.

"It's good for her lungs to sit up in a chair once in a while."

I go to mom and she is nearly in tears. "They won't let me get back in bed," she complains in her hoarse voice.

I hold her hand and talk with her, explaining what the nurse told me. Within a few minutes they are ready to get her back to the bed. As soon as her head hits the pillow she is asleep. Sitting up really took it out of her.

I sit next to her in the chair. I ask the nurse for some ice for my wrist. When she comes back, she says she thinks it might be broken and that I should get it x-rayed. I sit with the ice on it for about 20 minutes and then decide she's right.

I go down to the ER and find out it's not broken, just really sprained and bruised. I go back up and check on mom, who's still fast asleep so I head back home.

Thursday

They have decided to send mom to a specialty hospital until she is strong enough to come home. She will probably be transferred tomorrow. She is not well enough to go to a rehab facility yet and she still needs special care, since she is still receiving blood and cannot eat normally yet.

Today she has graduated to applesauce, however, and she is thrilled to be getting different food. She is still getting most of her nutrition through her IV, since she can't eat enough to sustain herself yet. She is also able to eat a special sherbet that is high in protein, carbs, and other vitamins and minerals. It's orange flavored and she really likes it.

She looks stronger than ever now and her voice, though rough from the continuing sore throat, is much better. She is sitting in the recliner more often today, although she hates it. Her head is still heavy and holding it up exhausts her.

Friday

Mom is at the new facility now and it is a wonderful place. I have a little longer drive, but it is so worth it to see her getting better. The staff is wonderful.

Mom is eating more often now. Her diet still consists of yogurt, applesauce, small milkshakes, and the nutritional sorbets. They are thickening her water so she can drink it, because she is unable to swallow thin liquids yet.

She is staying in their ICU until she no longer needs blood. They continue to adjust her meds, trying to stop the little bleed.

It's been five days and she is finally off the plasma, which means they have her meds correct now. She is finally eating soft foods like cottage cheese and scrambled eggs and she can now have water and coffee that has not been thickened. She is really happy about that! She is moved out of ICU and into a regular room.

The days pass quickly and after being at the specialty hospital for three more weeks, she is finally strong enough to come home.

Summer passes quickly into Fall and mom is doing great. Her heart doctor put her on a list for a special study. They are using volunteers to test a new porcine (pig) valve to replace damaged ones. Since mom's valve is also bad, she is a good candidate.

Deborah Alyne Christy

Chapter 21

"That which does not kill us makes us stronger."
Friedrich Nietzsche

My cousin Karen has returned from Scotland and has come to see us. After visiting for two days, she is getting ready to leave for the airport. She is returning to California to continue her work.

Mom is experiencing a heaviness in her chest, so I give her a nitroglycerin tablet to put under her tongue. Karen will be upstairs with her luggage any minute, so I head out to the garage to take something out of the freezer for dinner.

My head is deep inside the freezer when the door flies open and Karen looks frantic.

"Deb! Your mom passed out!"

"What?!" I fly into the house and mom is on the floor of her bedroom, unconscious. I can't wake her, so I hit the lifeline panic button that she's wearing. I stroke her hair, trying to wake her while waiting for the operator to come on the line.

It's been over a minute and now I am panicking. I grab the phone and dial 911 and someone answers right away. I am explaining everything when the lifeline operator finally answers. Now I am trying to talk to both of them. The 911 operator tells me to disconnect the lifeline operator, so I do.

She has sent the paramedics and is keeping me on the line to get more information. I am looking at mom and I can see that she just missed hitting her head on the bookcase. I shake my head at the luck of it all.

Just as the fire department arrives, she begins to stir. Four gorgeous firemen surround her as I tell them about her heart issues. She is getting more awake as they try to speak with her. They want her to go to the hospital, but she doesn't want to go. I encourage her to go, saying that I have no idea what happened, but she argues with us.

When they try to lift her to a seated position, she cries out in pain and grabs her leg. They look at her leg and it looks like her ankle is broken. Now they are really pushing for her to go in the ambulance, which just arrived. She relents when she realizes she can't walk.

I assure Karen it is okay for her to go, since she is in danger of missing her flight. We hug for a long time, the she heads out.

Mom's ankle is broken and they want to keep her over night because of the fainting spell. We finally get it all worked out. Mom is not supposed to get up when she takes the nitroglycerin, because it drops her blood pressure. That's why she fainted.

It's obvious mom can't use her walker with a broken ankle, so she heads back to Life Care so they can help her and start physical therapy as soon as she can put weight on her leg. Meanwhile, I arrange to get her a wheelchair and a bedside commode in hopes of getting her home sooner.

It takes three weeks for her to be strong enough to come home and even then, we use the wheelchair whenever we leave the house.

Mom is accepted into the porcine valve study and we start going to Spokane regularly for the testing that's involved to make sure she is a good candidate and will survive the surgery. One test is an echocardiogram to make sure her stent is working, which she does in February.

When we return a week later to go over all of the test results, we are informed that they have discovered a spot on her lung and they think it might be cancer. They cannot continue the study for her until she has a biopsy.

Oh dear, here we go again!

We see a doctor in town, who was one of the

doctors I met on the night they put in mom's stent. He takes the biopsy the next day. It is a painful procedure, because they have to go through the back to get to the lung. Mom is uncomfortable afterwards and I am extremely nervous.

We hear back from the doctor the next day and find out that it is cancer and it needs to be removed. We make an appointment to see him and he tells us that he has been in touch with the doctors from the study.

"I believe your heart will not survive the surgery, so I have convinced your doctors to keep you in the study. You will have the best chance of survival if your valve is repaired beforehand."

"How long do we wait after the heart surgery before you take out the cancer?" I ask him. "Don't we have to worry about it metastasizing?"

"Yes that is a concern. I will want to perform the surgery about eight weeks later. I can't remove the cancer, since the lung is spongy and there is no way to stitch it up from the inside. Our only choice is to remove a portion of the lung itself."

"Will I be short of breath?"

"That is a possibility."

Mom doesn't like the sound of that—

especially after watching dad struggle for breath in his last weeks.

After weeks of testing, mom is ready for the valve operation. It's set for May 18th, so I talk with Darlene about watching Molly during the day.

Darlene met a great guy last fall and she moved in with him this spring. He lives in Spokane Valley, which is on the way to the hospital. He has three dogs, so Molly will have a chance to play.

Once again, mom asked the doctors not to 'crack' her chest and they assured her that they can do it without opening her up.

The surgery day arrives and we get her checked in at 6:30 in the morning. Surgery is set for 8:30. I am able to visit with her once she has been all prepped for a little while and then I am taken to a waiting area.

I downloaded Netflix and a couple of games onto my iPhone to keep my mind occupied, so I find a corner and put in my ear buds. There is a desk near the entrance to the waiting room where a lady answers the phone from the doctors, so I make sure I am facing her.

I get a call from Dr. Roberts after about an hour and he lets me know everything is going well and they are about a third of the way through. Two hours pass without word, and I am feeling nervous. She should be about done by now. 30 minutes later, Dr. Roberts comes to get me and takes me out into the hall.

"Everything went well and we were planning to finish up when we encountered a problem. There is a small, flexible wire we use during the surgery to guide the valve. Something happened that we have never seen before. The wire brushed your mom's heart and created a tiny nick. We have been waiting nearly an hour for the nick to stop oozing blood, but it is not stopping.

"We don't want to keep her like this much longer. If the bleeding doesn't stop soon we will have to stitch it up. There is only one way to do that: we have to open her up. There is no other way."

I nod, feeling terrible for mom. This is what she absolutely did not want. "How much longer will you wait?"

"We will give it another hour. I will be back to update you then. We will need your approval to go ahead, since you are her durable power of attorney."

"Okay."

I spend the hour fretting over the turn of events. The doctor returns as promised and informs me they have to proceed, since the bleeding will not stop.

"I feel terrible about this. I know your mom was very much against it. The worst part about it is that it only needs one stitch!"

"Seriously? That is really sad. Go ahead and do what you must to get her finished. You have my approval."

"Give us about an hour to finish up. I'll be back to let you know how it went."

"Okay, thank you Dr. Roberts."

This has been a very long day and I will be glad when it's over.

Mom is finally in her room and she is doing well, considering she is in a lot of pain from having her chest opened up and her ribcage cracked and spread open.

After five days she is transferred to Life Care in Coeur d'Alene where she will spend about three weeks.

I spend the afternoons with her. I bring my laptop and hook it up to her TV. We stream Netflix or I bring a DVD. After we have dinner together I head home.

Life Care is one place that allows you to bring pets as long as their shots are up to date, so I always bring Molly with me. I keep water and food bowls in mom's room, along with a travel bed I have for her.

Molly loves to walk the hallways and get petted by everyone. She is such a well-behaved dog that the staff loves her and doesn't mind her visiting other patients. Even their house cat, also named Molly, doesn't mind her.

We visit the pulmonary doctor mid-June and he wants to plan the surgery for her lung cancer for July 3rd. It seems so soon after mom's heart surgery, but he doesn't want to take the chance that the cancer will change or spread.

Poor mom, she has been through so much this last year. We agree with the date and we head home.

July 3rd arrives quickly. Once again, I am waiting for the surgery to finish. At least her surgery is at Kootenai Medical Center, the hospital in Coeur d'Alene. It makes it easier for me to pop home and care for Molly every few hours.

When I am finally able to join mom in her room, she looks gray and her face is contorted in pain. They warned us that lung surgery is the most painful surgery, but neither of us was prepared for her level of pain.

"I hurt so much," she whispered as I stroked her hair.

I went to find her nurse right away. They set her up with a morphine pump, but she is too weak at first to use it and I am not allowed to do it for her. So the patient nurses come in every couple of hours when I call them. The staff at KMC is hand picked and they are always wonderful.

Mom is in severe pain for her entire stay at the hospital. The long scar down her back and the muscles that are trying to knit back together make it nearly impossible for her to lie on her back at all, so the nurses shift her position often. At first, they had a wedge to keep her off of the incision. After two or three days they switch it to pillows, which is more comfortable.

She goes to Life Care again after five days. She is laying on her back more, but it is painful and she gets pain medication regularly. This is unusual since mom hates to take pain medication and usually puts it off as long as possible.

Life settles down after a few months and we

are delighted that mom is not short of breath all the time. She only struggles when she has been on her feet too long, but most of that is the pain in her low back. We had hoped the hip replacement was going to alleviate that pain, but it didn't.

Chapter 22

"The two hardest tests on the spiritual road are the patience to wait for the right moment and the courage not to be disappointed with what we encounter." Paulo Coelho

As mom improves, I start working on this book as time allows. I feel blocked toward the end and my ongoing depression is getting worse.

I have struggled with depression from the time I was a little girl. I started taking antidepressants when Jennifer started really acting out, which only partially helped. Over the years, my doctor tried putting me on additional antidepressants, but I could never handle all of the side effects.

In desperation, I see my doctor again. She suggests I try hypnotherapy. Wow! I have never thought of that. I wonder if it will help…particularly since I can't hear Johanna anymore.

I get online and start looking for someone, not expecting to find a hypnotherapist in town. I am surprised to find that there are several people. I look them all over, going to any with websites and stop at one in particular: Journey to Wellness. I get a warm feeling on her site and decide to give her a call. I'm not sure how I'll pay for it, but I have to at least try.

When Jackie calls me back, I instantly know she is the right one for me. I explain my financial situation and she offers me a cash discount. I decide to go for it, even if it means paying each of my monthly bills a few dollars less each month. I always pay more than the minimum charges, so I should have no problem.

I am delighted when I meet Jackie. She is warm and wonderful and I love her energy. As we talk I notice we are very similar in our spiritual beliefs. I decide that I want her to really know me before I try the hypnotherapy, so we have three counseling sessions first.

Finally, after a month, I am ready for the hypnotherapy. I have doubts as to whether it can work or not, but any insight into this life-long depression can only be a benefit.

I don't feel very different while under hypnosis, except that I feel very focused; there is peacefulness and a calm that I can't explain. We work down through the years to get closer to whatever has me in such a terrible place. No matter how far back I go, I still feel this sense of loss and aloneness that has plagued my all of my life.

Suddenly, without any warning, I get a huge revelation. "Oh my God!" I exclaim loudly.

"Tell me," Jackie responds quietly.

"I was a twin and Johanna was my sister! But she was lost when mom's body was trying to abort the pregnancy. *That's* the sense of loss I have always felt! It makes so much sense now! I survived but she didn't.

"We were supposed to make a difference in the world together—together. But after she was lost I was lost, too. I have been trying to get back to her ever since without even knowing it."

After Jackie brings me out of hypnosis, my head is spinning at the realizations. I am having trouble wrapping my mind around it.

"Did I just make that whole thing up?"

"What do *you* think?"

I shake my head. "It feels accurate."

"Then it is."

I went home and told mom about the session, trying to see if she thought there was any truth to it. I'm not sure how mom will respond, since she doesn't believe in the same things that I do.

"You know," she starts, "I kept trying to abort you. I've told you about this, since I think that the DES Stilboestrol drug they gave me to keep from losing you is responsible for your ovarian problems."

I nod that I remember and she continues.

"The reason the doctor put me on the drug was because I started to bleed and cramp and we were sure I was going to lose you. I wonder if that's when it happened..."

Mom drifts off in thought and I am surprised that she is even considering the possibility that I may have been a twin.

Several days have passed and I am still digesting this new information. One thing is certain, however: I am no longer depressed! I truly feel differently. It's like a weight has been lifted from my life and I can breathe and feel again.

I have tried to meditate so I can ask Johanna about the hypnosis and my realization, but haven't succeeded yet. I am sinking into the bathtub and decide to try again. But my mind won't quiet down and I have a stupid song stuck on auto-loop in my head.

"Johanna! I want to reach you but I can't keep my mind on the white light."

"I'm here, dear one."

"What? You can come to me without meditating?"

"Of course. It is only you who believes otherwise. You have been convinced that you need to meditate to speak with me and your other guides. We are always here, listening."

I let out a big sigh. "You could have told me that."

"I have. You chose not to listen. That way, you don't have to accept the blame for not reaching us."

"Blame?"

"Think about it. Is that not what you do when you are unable to meditate? You give up, believing you cannot get to us. Actually, you were not willing to reach us. You did not want to let go of the untruth you had created."

"I do fight it sometimes, don't I?"

"Indeed."

"I want to talk to you about my hypnotherapy session. I felt you were there along with the other guides."

"We were. We were holding the space for you so you felt safe."

"Is it true? Were we sisters?"

"It is true."

"Then why didn't you ever tell me? It could have made a difference so much sooner. Maybe I wouldn't have wasted so many years in this stupid depression."

"It was not my place to tell you. Do you truly believe that it would have made a difference in the past? Do you believe you were in the right place emotionally and spiritually to understand the significance?"

"Yes, I think so…I don't understand, Johanna."

"When you sought out Jackie, what was your intention?"

"To figure out once and for all why I have spent my entire life depressed and not wanting to be here. It was one of the final keys to understand. I've done everything else."

"Exactly! You have done everything else. This understanding is like a puzzle that you had to fit together before you could find and assimilate the last piece."

"So I wasn't ready to know you yet?" I ask incredulously.

"Close your eyes. Think back to when you first heard me. Think about hearing who I am. What is your reaction?"

"I find it interesting and cool...but that's all."

"Would the knowledge have aided you in any way?"

"No."

"Does the knowledge aid you now?"

"Yes it does." I nod in comprehension. I open my eyes and look at her and smile. It makes sense now. It *all* makes sense now.

"Johanna, I am thinking that I might be able to decrease my depression meds now...what do *you* think? One of the reasons I have stayed on them is that it has helped with the extreme highs and lows of the cyclic depression—known as bipolar — that I have experienced."

"You need not fear reducing your antidepressants. What you call a cyclic depression is merely your mind triggering your emotions around a past event that you have not healed.

"But I have done the forgiveness and releasing."

"Apparently, there is more to forgive and release. If there was not, then you would not be suffering."

"But isn't it a chemical imbalance in the brain?"

"Perhaps. Do you not feel that you can heal that? Do you believe it is harder to heal that than it is to heal cancer or abuse or traumatic events?"

"I don't think so."

"Then search yourself for any lingering memories or pain that you have not healed. When you feel you have found them all, try decreasing your pills. If the bad feelings return, go back to the full dose and heal what surfaced. Continue this until you are able to decrease them without any ill effects."

"Okay. I know one of the issues I still face is money. I am beginning to wonder if the problem is that I have no reference for having plenty of money. We never had money in excess when I was a kid, and I have never had it regularly as an adult. I don't know how to *feel* about money."

"You say you have no reference for attracting money into your life because it has not existed in your life regularly. You do not need a reference to have money and success in your life. You only need to love. Love the fear that drives money away. Love the anxiety you feel in your chest when you do not have enough. Love and forgive yourself for not knowing how to do this in the past. Activate your early warning system so you are aware when fear is entering your thoughts."

"All right, I will. I wish I could go back to the way I was in the early 90s. I loved that time. I felt so connected to everything and everyone; and I was in contact with all of you regularly. I want to feel that way again."

"You cannot go back. There is only one direction that energy flows: forward. This does not mean that you cannot regain the connectedness—in fact, it is vitally important that you do. A time of great change is coming and you will play an active part in it. Your ability to love and to free others to love will be an important tool of this change."

"Johanna, I still have confusion around the idea of God. You know that I don't believe there is an entity who sits on high and judges each one of us. But so many people believe in it that I sometimes wonder if I'm right."

"What people refer to as God is not a supernatural being who looks down from Heaven and judges your actions. It *is* a presence, however, and that presence is Love. When a person's heart fills with feeling when praying or during times of great faith, what they are feeling is their connection to Love."

"That makes more sense to me."

As Johanna fades away with a smile, I call out to her: "I love you Johanna."

"You are loved in return," she answers before she vanishes.

Epilogue

"The purpose of life is to live it, to taste experience to the utmost, to reach out eagerly and without fear for newer and richer experience." Eleanor Roosevelt

It seems the more I grow and learn, the more I *need* to learn. Each phase of growth and development challenges my old core beliefs and revs up my psyche. It can be difficult to live with intention, because I can't blame anything on anyone else. I must take responsibility for every action and reaction.

Johanna and Sananda still walk with me and talk with me when I let them. Sometimes I find that I try to shut them out, because living in the constant search for truth can be overwhelming.

There are times of great upheaval in my life, when it feels like I'm going to hit bottom spiritually. I call it falling into the void. Every time I have that experience it ends up being the most incredible time of healing and growth for me. It's like undergoing tiny rebirths of truth throughout my entire life.

One thing that makes it easier now is the fact that my depression has never returned. I haven't gotten off of the pills entirely, but I am getting closer all the time.

I love this life and the opportunities I have

been given to share what I'm learning with others. If providing this insight into me helps others heal, then I gladly accept it and share it with you.